"Jennifer Levin's book, *The Traumatic Loss Workbook*, promises to be extremely helpful in offering the reader a way to process and understand their response to sudden loss. Every page offers compassion, guidance, and information to support one through a very painful journey. I highly recommend it."

—**Pamela D. Blair, PhD**, coauthor of *I Wasn't Ready to Say Goodbye* and *The Long Grief Journey*

"A beautiful and important guide for anyone who has experienced sudden loss, *The Traumatic Loss Workbook* is full of practical guidance and comfort, walking grievers through what's most helpful immediately and over time. I'll be gifting this book on repeat."

—**Tina Payne Bryson, PhD**, *New York Times* bestselling coauthor of *The Whole-Brain Child*, and founder of The Center for Connection

"Jennifer Levin's *The Traumatic Loss Workbook* reads like you suddenly have a needed, wise, support coach—quietly guiding you toward more healing. Jennifer writes with authority and a pragmatic, purposeful approach. She takes the multifaceted complexity of traumatic grief and guides the reader with clear explanations and helpful workbook exercises. What makes the workbook even more unique is she writes it with a warmth and compassion that safely guides the reader in their grief healing journey. I wish I had had this book when I suffered my traumatic grief losses, yet even now, years later, I got tremendous benefit from reading it."

—**Kim Cantin**, speaker/author, mudslide survivor, and author of *Where Yellow Flowers Bloom*

"Jennifer Levin and this book literally saved my life. Distinguishing between trauma and grief was the high point of the book. The exercises allowed me to process trauma and arrive at a place where I could grieve. The workbook format is genius. It enabled me to do the exercises I could handle, and save the painful ones for later. This book is a tool for untangling yourself."

—**Prudence Fenton**, award-winning creative visualist; and founder of the Willis, Wonderland Foundation which educates the songwriters of the next generation

"Navigating a changed world after the sudden death of a loved one can be a lonely road with unexpected twists and turns. Jennifer Levin's workbook provides guidance and assurance: You are not alone. You can find your way through grief and uncertainty. The exercises are designed to assist and support you, with the wisdom of someone who has listened to, and learned from, the lives of many bereaved people."

—**Donna Schuurman, EdD**, senior director of advocacy and education, and executive director emeritus at the Dougy Center: The National Grief Center for Children & Families

"Countless counselors offer bereavement support as part of their services, but very few have the specialized skills and extensive experience to offer guidance to those whose lives have been shattered by the suicide, homicide, fatal accident, or other tragic death of a loved one. This is what makes Jennifer Levin's remarkable workbook such a welcome companion on the healing journey through traumatic loss. With clarity and compassion grounded in decades of collaboration with survivors, she offers wise counsel and practical steps to soothe a troubled spirit, learn the lessons of loss, and reconstruct life in the wake of profound decimation. I literally will recommend it to every client I serve who stands in the shadow of such loss, looking for a light to guide them toward a life that again has meaning."

—**Robert A. Neimeyer, PhD**, director of the Portland Institute for Loss and Transition, and author of *Living Beyond Loss*

"Jennifer Levin's book genuinely and caringly expresses the dialectic of both acceptance and change for those confronted with sudden loss and traumatic grief. She offers a guide through the process that respects individual differences. This book will be helpful to those grieving, and to professionals working with traumatic grief."

—**Patricia Gieselman, LMFT**, director for Choices Counseling & Skills Center, specializing in dialectical behavior therapy (DBT); and DBT-Linehan Board of Certification-certified clinician

The

Traumatic Loss Workbook

Powerful Skills for
Navigating the Grief Caused by
a Sudden or Unexpected Death

JENNIFER R. LEVIN, PHD, LMFT

New Harbinger Publications, Inc.

Copyright © 2025 by Jennifer R. Levin
           New Harbinger Publications, Inc.
           5720 Shattuck Avenue
           Oakland, CA 94609
           www.newharbinger.com

Cover design by Amy Daniel

Acquired by Jennye Garibaldi

Edited by Iris van de Pavert

Library of Congress Cataloging-in-Publication Data on file

Printed in the United States of America

27   26   25

10   9   8   7   6   5   4   3   2   1   First Printing

To my mom, Nancy Mary Levin, thank you for being my rock, foundation, and dearest friend. You mean the world to me, and I cherish you more than words can convey

and

To all the clients I have worked with, who have graciously allowed me to share in their deepest pain and trusted me to help them navigate the journey of adapting and finding hope, as they continue to live without their loved ones.

Contents

Foreword

You have probably never experienced a pain greater than the grief resulting from a sudden or unexpected death. One day, you are living life with your loved one, and in an instant, they are gone. Living with this pain, when there was no chance to share any words during the dying act, or reliving the horrific circumstances of a traumatic or violent dying is surreal, and the experience can seem insurmountable. You may be feeling as if you have been left suspended in an unspoken conversation with no opportunity for a final goodbye embrace.

My career as a clinician and researcher has given me tremendous insight into the lives of patients living in the aftermath of a traumatic death. You may experience not only the emotional pain of separation distress, such as longing for your loved one, but also traumatic distress that includes intrusive memories, avoidance of reminders of their death, and symptoms of hyperarousal.

As a result, relief from the pain associated with a violent or traumatic death may feel impossible for you. There is an enormous need for effective and innovative means to ease and manage your debilitating pain, such as the resources found in the descriptive title of this workbook, "powerful skills for navigating the grief caused by a sudden or unexpected death." This interactive workbook addresses your needs with expertise and emotional sensitivity.

This traumatic grief workbook is a fundamental tool for understanding and managing the difficulties of finding and creating comfort after you have experienced a loss of this caliber. And workbooks such as this are rare and long overdue. Few restoring words exist to offer solace for those grieving such deeply personal losses. Traumatic grief requires a practical, adaptive plan to reestablish a calming and coherent connection with your loved one.

Jennifer's work provides such a plan. Her inspiration for an imaginal retelling of your story and your loss and revising the narrative of a dreadful death allows you to commemorate the life of your loved one, and are among the gifts of Jennifer's experience and expertise.

I first met Jennifer in Seattle while volunteering with her to organize a peer-led companioning and group support service for loved ones experiencing a sudden or violent death. The program highlighted Jennifer's skills as a seasoned lecturer, consultant, and trainer. As a therapist, she has extensive experience with those disabled by traumatic grief after sudden or violent dying. Her knowledge and compassion are notable; demonstrated by her caring and concern, foundational practices, and ability to hold space for taxing emotions associated with the stages of grief.

Writing a traumatic grief workbook incorporating such a unique combination of trauma and grief is a challenging prospect. Her guidance is a simplified and informed plan for traumatic grief and provides a reassuring, comprehensive text that can be read and applied at home over and again. The ordered chapters provide a restorative structure of time, space, and action for traumatic grief through descriptions and guided exercises. These pages are filled with pertinent advice and counseling that can be read and applied at any point during your traumatic grief journey.

There is an ennobling quality to this workbook, incorporating hope and action. Traumatic grief needs a practical, adaptive plan to restore a calming and coherent connection with your loved one. An imaginal retelling of your traumatic experience allows you to honor the life of your loved one and revise the narrative of their dying.

This workbook creates a space for celebrating the life of your loved one and moving beyond the horrible circumstances of their death. But it also provides direction and guidance for rebuilding your life with meaning by incorporating the presence of your loved one in your daily life. In other words, integrating the love and absence of your loved one within the felt presence of their spirit. There is no doubt, *The Traumatic Loss Workbook: Powerful Skills for Navigating the Grief Caused by a Sudden or Unexpected Death* can be a source of direction and hope during one of life's most challenging encounters.

—Edward K. Rynearson, M.D.
Emeritus Clinical Professor of Psychiatry
University of Washington
Seattle, Washington

Introduction:
Welcome to a Safe Place

If your loved one has died in a sudden or unexpected manner, you know there are no words sufficient to describe your grief and pain. After a traumatic loss, it is common to experience a host of complex feelings, including disbelief; an unending well of yearning and sadness; and symptoms of trauma, such as anxiety or hypervigilance. Some of your days may feel manageable, but every day, especially early on, presents itself with its own set of challenges. At times, the emotional weight may feel overwhelming. It may also seem like no one truly grasps the depth of your pain, leaving you to feel isolated or alone in your experience.

I am so glad you have found this workbook and that you have found the help you need. I am also truly sorry that you find yourself in a position to need its message and tools in your life. I have been working with individuals living with sudden and unexpected death for more than 30 years. Not only am I a traumatic grief therapist, but I have also personally experienced the sudden and unexpected death of clients and loved ones. I get it. As you so painfully know, while we cannot change the past, we can change how we respond to our present circumstances.

I wrote this book because your needs after a sudden or unexpected death are above and beyond the norm. I wanted you to have a resource dedicated to your experience. Countless numbers of clients have expressed frustrations over the well-meaning but misguided attempts of family and friends who compare their grief due to deaths from chronic illness or natural causes to your traumatic grief. While all grief is undeniably painful, the trauma and complexities associated with sudden, unexpected loss introduce challenges that are often beyond the grasp of those who haven't experienced such trauma. This book aims to address those additional layers of suffering you are experiencing, with the depth and understanding you deserve.

Unfortunately, there are not a lot of resources tailored to sudden and unexpected deaths. Grief is a natural response to loss, and the pain you're experiencing after your loved one's traumatic death is a normal part of this process. It's important to remember that grieving doesn't mean you are broken. This workbook validates your experience and connects you with realities that others in your circumstances also experience. After a traumatic loss, it is common to seek support from a professional with expertise in this area. At present, there are not an abundance of mental health professionals who specialize in sudden or unexpected death. If you work with a therapist who does not have that specific expertise, you can incorporate the exercises from this book into your work together. You or your therapist can also download additional resources designed to accompany this workbook at http://www.newharbinger.com/54926.

This workbook addresses your exceptional needs as you learn to adjust to the complexity of your life without your loved one. It has been crafted to offer you a safe space to address your pain while equipping you with essential skills for navigating the complex issues associated with a sudden or unexpected death. It provides you with a sanctuary for exploring the entire continuum of traumatic grief, offering guidance and pathways for hope and creating a meaningful future. The information and exercises target grief due to health crises, suicides, overdoses, accidents, homicides, natural disasters, acts of terrorism, or military action. Since many of these specific topics are touched upon only briefly, I strongly encourage you to explore the additional resources listed at the back of the book for a deeper understanding of your particular situation.

How to Use This Book

This workbook is written for those of you who have experienced the sudden or unexpected death of a loved one, regardless of the amount of time that has passed since your loss. If your loved one's death was more recent, the first chapters will resonate more strongly with your current situation, but reading the later chapters will hold space for where you are going. If you are further out in your grief, the beginning chapters will highlight your growth and provide tools for difficult moments of intense grief that continue to occur, and the latter chapters will speak more clearly to where you are in time. The workbook is most useful when read more than once, and several of the exercises are available to download at http://www.newharbinger.com/54926 so you can complete them multiple times.

I recommend reading the workbook in chronological order. Chapters 1–3 focus on stabilization of trauma symptoms that often occur after a traumatic loss. True grief work cannot begin until your body and mind are in a calm, safe state. I encourage you to take as much time as you need with these chapters before moving on to chapter 4. You will use a symptom assessment and chapter exercises to deepen your learning, and a grief diary to help monitor and track your progress. When you engage in these exercises, try and find a comfortable place, free from distractions, where you can connect with your thoughts and emotions. Although incredibly difficult and painful, there is so much insight you can gain about yourself, your relationships with others, your values, and the future you want to create through this journey. I invite you to sit with the material, tolerate the feelings as they arise, and honor the process.

Thank You for Trusting Me

The traumatic death of your loved one will most likely be one of the most difficult things you will ever experience. Your pain and love story are intimate and perhaps one of the most personal aspects of your being. Trusting something or someone with this personal experience, being willing and open to bearing your soul, and practicing vulnerability may seem like an overwhelming task.

I am in awe of and inspired by the clients who work with me after the sudden or unexpected death of their loved one. I feel privileged and honored knowing they have placed their trust in me, sharing their raw pain and private moments. By engaging in this book, you are willing to do the same. We have now entered a relationship, and I am going to help you create a safe place to work through your pain and grief. I can hold hope for your future when you can't. Thank you for trusting me as you move toward healing. Together, we will get through this, one step and one moment at a time.

—Jennifer

CHAPTER 1

Understand Your Traumatic Grief

The death of your loved one is a traumatic, life-changing experience. But it is not a life-ending experience. In the immediate aftermath, your life became instantly unrecognizable, overridden with pain, sadness, and complex grief needs. You may have felt or continue to feel unsafe. You may have experienced or continue to experience intense symptoms of trauma and grief as you struggle with basic tasks. Friends and family may not understand your grief, and, as a result, it may be immensely challenging to get the support you need from others. You may feel isolated and alone or find yourself searching for information about how to cope with your grief and trauma. This chapter provides an overview of the complex and interwoven factors that contribute to pain, grief, and trauma. And although your circumstances are unique, understanding how sudden and unexpected death is different from other types of death, along with the factors that may shape your reaction, will empower you to process, cope, and navigate the life-long relationship you have entered with your traumatic grief.

You never expect someone you love to die suddenly or unexpectedly. While it may be impossible to predict how long our time on earth will be, we are all eventually confronted with the reality of our mortality. Most of us rarely dwell on our own death, often hoping it will come in a natural, painless manner. When loved ones pass away in anticipated or foreseeable circumstances, the grief is profound and difficult, yet it differs significantly in intensity and nature from the overwhelming shock and pain you are experiencing now.

This book was written to support your unique needs as a griever who experienced the *sudden* or *unexpected* death of your loved one. You may be a grieving parent, raw with emotion and unspeakable pain after the death of your child. A spouse or partner overwhelmed with grief after the traumatic passing of your soulmate. A family member traumatized and lost after the demise of your parent, sibling, or other close relation. Traumatic grief can occur after experiencing the death of someone you love due to an unexpected medical crisis, accident, suicide, homicide, or substance overdose. Traumatic grief can also result from a natural disaster, terrorist act, military action, or war. Your loved one's death may have been sudden and unexpected, sudden but not unexpected, or unexpected but not sudden.

- **Sudden and unexpected deaths** include aneurysms, fatal heart attacks that happen to people with no known heart problems, fatal accidents, suicides without warning, and mass shootings.

- **Deaths that are sudden but not unexpected** involve individuals living with chronic health conditions, those struggling with drug or alcohol use, or loved ones who have had previous suicide attempts and then complete a suicide.

- **Unexpected deaths that are not sudden** encompass accidents, shootings, or health crises that caused a loved one to be placed on life support that was later terminated, which resulted in a prolonged ending.

Whether your loved one's death was sudden and/or unexpected, it was most likely overwhelming and traumatic in nature. You have probably figured out by now, there is no timeline when it comes to grieving. A traumatic death that occurred a month ago can be just as devastating as one that occurred three or ten years ago. If your loss recently occurred, you are in an acute phase of grief, but you may also be in the protective bubble of shock, numbness, and denial. As you continue in life, you will most likely be confronted with grief attacks, trauma symptoms, or unexpected triggers, especially during special events, holidays, anniversaries, or stressful times. This workbook provides you with techniques and tools to cope with the acute grief in the immediate aftermath of your loss, as well as providing you with the skills to utilize during your lifetime relationship with your traumatic grief.

Common Realities You May Face

There are many realities contributing to the different needs and challenges you may be experiencing. Because the death of your loved one was a highly personalized experience, not all of the common realities listed below may apply to your current situation.

Your Life Changed Instantly

The moment you learned your loved one died, your life forever changed. You may have been with your loved one when the death occurred, or you may have been notified by phone, in person, or by other means. But that moment will be etched in your mind forever. It changed who you were at your core and your life domains, which include work or school, physical and mental health, relationships with family and friends, intimate or romantic relationships, the environment where you live, financial resources, fun and recreation, spiritual/religious beliefs and personal growth. It affected the way you perceive the world, how others treat you, and what brings you meaning, purpose, and joy. Immediately, you were overcome with intense pain, grief, and shock. There may have been or currently exist feelings of numbness and denial. The amount of disruption and chaos in your life depends on your circumstances, but this experience will challenge your fundamental assumptions about the life you built, the relationships that support you, and your existence in the world.

The Experience May Have Caused a Trauma Response

You may be experiencing symptoms of trauma after your loved one's death for multiple reasons, including:

- Your loved one died in a violent way, or you perceived their body was harmed or they suffered.

- You witnessed your loved one die or found your loved one after death.

- You provided life-sustaining measures, made end-of-life decisions, or read police reports or stories that included details about your loved one's death.

However, not everyone who experiences the sudden or unexpected death of a loved one will develop symptoms of trauma.

Common trauma symptoms include: flashbacks, nightmares, rumination (replaying events over and over in your mind), anxiety, hypervigilance (waiting for the other shoe to drop), and other responses that interfere with your daily functioning. Unfortunately, these trauma symptoms are in addition to the grief you are feeling for your loved one. Chapter 2 will provide an in-depth explanation of traumatic grief and includes tools to cope with and stabilize intense trauma symptoms.

There Was an Inability to Say Goodbye

You were robbed of the chance to say goodbye to your loved one. There were no opportunities for final conversations or a chance to "get your affairs in order." When death arrives without warning and is out of the natural life order, there is no chance to express final sentiments. You may be living with words left unsaid. It is common to spend a significant amount of time preoccupied with your final conversation with your loved one, which may now seem meaningless and insufficient. Sometimes the last conversations are transactional texts like, "can you pick up something at the store," or a quick voicemail. These final exchanges can feel very empty, and for some people, final communications are not always positive interactions, which may complicate the grieving process even more.

You Have Many Unanswered Questions and Unknowns

The wake of your loved one's death may be full of unanswered questions or uncertainties. Your mind may be in overdrive trying to figure out the details related to their death. Circumstances dependent, it is common to focus your efforts on understanding everything that happened, how it happened, and why it happened. You may feel desperate to make sense of a situation that does not make sense. In searching for answers to the unknown, you may begin to question your role in your loved one's death. With so many unknowns, it is easy to wonder if your loved one would still be alive if you had done something differently. Guilt, self-blame, and regret often come into play along with thoughts such as, *I should have, I could have,* or *I wish I would have.* These are all coping mechanisms for dealing with the unknowns and unanswered questions.

The Death May Have Been Preventable

You may believe that your loved one's death was preventable, which can torment and complicate your grieving process. Depending on the circumstances, deaths that may have been preventable can result in anger, depression, and other intense emotions. Your grief may also be intermixed with guilt, blame (self or others), regret, or shame. Unfortunately, it is often not possible to confirm with certainty if the death could have been avoided, delayed, or changed if the circumstances were different.

If your loved one's death was recent, understanding your realities is a new process and may still be forthcoming. To guide your future grief work in this guidebook, answer the following questions about *the circumstances of your loved one*'s death according to each reality you experienced. If one of the realities does not apply to your circumstances, leave it blank. There is additional space for you to add a different reality that may better resonate with your situation.

How has your life instantly changed?

_____

_____

_____

_____

_____

What was traumatic about your experience?

_____

_____

_____

_____

What were the circumstances that contributed to your inability to say goodbye?

_____

_____

_____

_____

Describe your unanswered questions and unknowns.

_____

_____

_____

_____

Do you feel your loved one's death may have been preventable? If so, describe how.

_____

_____

_____

_____

_____

Write about any additional realities you are living with in the space below.

_____

_____

_____

_____

_____

Identifying your realities is a good starting point to understanding your grief and pain. Over time, as things become clearer and present themselves in new ways, I invite you to return to this exercise.

The Loss of the Assumptive World

After a traumatic death, it is common to feel vulnerable, a loss of control, unsafe, fearful, or an increased worry for loved ones. I have had many clients describe themselves as "going crazy," or report that "the rug has been pulled out from underneath them," after their loved one died. These feelings often stem from the shattering of the assumptive world, a world you may not even have known to exist, but it shattered when challenged by a traumatic event.

The *assumptive world* is an abstract world you create within yourself. It serves as an internal manual or guide to organize your beliefs and helps to interpret the world you live in. It contains the way you view yourself and others and creates a sense of stability, purpose, and meaning in your life (Janoff-Bulman 1992; Kauffman 2002). Your assumptive world contributes to your ability to navigate each day, trusting that you will remain safe, your needs will be fulfilled, and you can plan for your future. It offers a sense of control, fairness, and order that is immediately shattered after the sudden or unexpected death of your loved one. The *shattered assumptions theory* identifies three primary assumptions often shattered when a person is faced with a traumatic event (Janoff-Bulman 1992):

- **The world is benevolent.** The world and community you live in is a positive place filled with good people with upright intentions who can be trusted.

- **The world is meaningful.** Life has a sense of order. It is fair and purposeful, and you can protect yourself from negative consequences with your actions.

- **You are worthy.** You believe in your value and what you deserve in life. You are worthy of positive outcomes.

Once your assumptions have been shattered, you experience the world through new eyes. Highly dependent on the circumstances of your loss, it is common to find your world no longer seems like a kind, caring place. It lacks meaning and order, causing you to question beliefs about yourself and what you deserve. You may have lost trust in others, feel powerless, or have experienced a loss of control because overnight your life now feels unsafe, and you no longer perceive any sense of goodwill or expect anything to work in your favor. You may feel betrayed or wronged. The predictability, order, and continuity of life may now feel meaningless. Life may no longer make sense. You may question the purpose of your efforts or realize that you are incapable of protecting yourself or those you love.

A sudden death can also cause you to question your self-worth and what you deserve in life or in your future. As a result, you may change the way you behave, interact with others, or engage with society at large. You may feel intense anxiety or an inability to sense what feels normal or real and be unable to function on a daily level. I have witnessed clients fearful of leaving the safety of their homes and reluctant to engage in everyday tasks that are associated with how their loved one died (like driving in a car or being in public settings). Others become overly protective of their loved ones and panic when family or friends do not answer their phones, reply to texts, or are late arriving home. The aftermath of the shattered assumptive world can be very scary, but most people find some comfort once they understand the rationale for their feelings and are able to take action to comfort themselves. You can create safety and stability with the tools described in the following chapters.

Rebuilding Your Assumptive World

Recreating your assumptive world is an important part of your healing experience. There are many ways to do this, but it will take time, patience, and compassion. Initial steps include:

- Acknowledging the assumptions in your world that have been shattered

- Reflecting on your belief system prior to your loved one's death

Only when you understand the disruptions in your perceptions about yourself, others, and the world you live in can you start to rebuild a new belief system and reestablish a new sense of trust and faith in yourself and others. Trauma and tragedy bring so much loss, but they can also bring out kindness and goodness in people, often from the ones you least expect. Over time, you will engage in new experiences and build new relationships that will create a new set of assumptions. This will allow you to feel safe again and supported in your life. Recognizing how your foundational beliefs have been shattered and actively taking steps to gradually rebuild your assumptive world can be an empowering experience.

Describe any assumptions that you now realize have been shattered.

_____

_____

_____

_____

_____

Moving Toward Healing

Although grief has no timeline and the pain of your loved one's absence may feel insurmountable, I promise you, *you will not always feel this way.* Throughout this workbook, you will notice I use the phrase "move toward healing." The truth is you will never fully heal from the sudden or unexpected death of your loved one. However, the pain and grief will inevitably change and evolve, and you will continually *move toward healing.* The grief and trauma symptoms will slowly subside, and the healthy memories of your loved one will grow stronger. Your ability to function and reengage with the world will slowly return, and you will redefine and rediscover feelings of contentment, joy, and peace. In Chapter 11, we will explore this concept in-depth.

The exercises in each chapter will help you track your progress, record your grief and trauma symptoms, and identify or create new ideas for your future that will continually move you toward healing. You may be in a headspace where thoughts of healing, future possibilities, and life without your loved one are undesirable or seem out of reach. That's completely understandable. Remaining open to the possibility that your feelings might evolve during or after completing the exercises can significantly aid your journey toward healing.

Despite the overwhelming grief, trauma, and pain you are currently experiencing, I want you to know there is hope and a way to create a meaningful future. Please understand that the process is slow, and you will need to be kind and gentle with yourself, but there are opportunities for insight and discovery along the way. I acknowledge and fully understand that you want nothing but the return of your loved one, and, oh, how I *wish* we had that option. I encourage you to use the information, skills, and tools in this workbook at your own pace. In time, you will be able to create a future that integrates the essence and memories of your loved one as you continue forward on your life path.

Chapter Highlights and Traumatic Grief Goals

You may find it helpful to document what you have learned in chapter 1 and identify goals. The concept of having goals for your grief may seem strange. When I begin working with clients, I found taking a minute to identify where you would like to experience realistic changes in how you feel, do, or think is beneficial.

Use the following space to document major concepts you learned in chapter 1.

Examples:

Unexpected death is not the same as a cancer death.

The death of my loved one changes how I feel around others.

The theory of shattered assumptions helps explain why I so often feel out of control.

_____

_____

_____

_____

_____

Use the space below to establish some initial goals at the onset of your grief journey using this workbook. Establishing these goals will help you track your progress and provide a direction for some of your work.

Examples:

To find a way to explain my grief to others that better represents my internal experience.

To develop skills to cope with intense moments of grief, trauma, and emotional pain.

To find hope for my future after my loved one's death.

To remain connected to my loved one in death.

_____

_____

_____

_____

Concluding Thoughts

Sometimes it can feel like you are not making any progress in grief or that your pain remains constant and unchanging. Reflecting back on your grief goals over time can be a beneficial experience and helpful reminder of the place where you started and the progress you have made along the way.

You have taken an important step in moving toward your healing by starting this workbook. The sudden or unexpected death of your loved one is life changing, but it is not life ending. The pain, grief, and trauma you are experiencing are so difficult, and your changes will most likely be slow. You will need an abundance of patience and kindness with yourself along the way to endure the journey you never asked to travel. But you have now started building the foundation of skills and resources you need to process, cope, and continue living with your grief.

CHAPTER 2

Surviving Beyond Your Worst Nightmare

You may feel like many others who describe the aftermath of their loved one's sudden or unexpected death as a horrific nightmare. When you wake in the morning, you might experience a fleeting moment of relief, as if nothing has happened, only to have the trauma of loss begin anew. There usually comes a time when it becomes undeniable: these new circumstances are not a fleeting nightmare, but your new reality. This is when the overwhelm and pain can become paralyzing. Not only is there heart-wrenching grief, but there also can be symptoms of trauma, which include fear, anxiety, intrusive memories, or intense, constantly changing and uncontrollable emotions. In this chapter, you will learn how your body processes and reacts to a traumatic event. You will be introduced to techniques to help regulate your emotions and establish safety and comfort in the immediate aftermath of your loved one's death. This chapter also includes an assessment to provide an ongoing opportunity for tracking any trauma symptoms you may be experiencing.

In the immediate aftermath of your loved one's death, it is common to experience a state of shock, numbness, or disbelief. You may feel flat, lifeless, or even nothing, because you have emotionally disconnected from your feelings to protect yourself from impending pain. Countless numbers of clients I have worked with described their initial traumatic grief experience as being engulfed in a protective bubble of traumatic shock or denial, before having to confront the reality of their loss. Others have referred to this time as a "safety wall" that separates the intellectual understanding of their loved one's death from the emotional difficulty of accepting and processing the loss.

It is a myth that trauma only happens to veterans who serve their country in war or individuals who experience a catastrophic life event, such as a tsunami or mass shooting. In fact, many of my clients are unaware they are experiencing both trauma and grief after their loved one's death. Trauma is not a disease. It is the way your body responds to an event that threatens your safety or life *or* the safety or life of someone you love. According to Peter Levine, PhD, trauma occurs when your ability to cope with a perceived threat is overwhelmed or compromised (Levine 2005). The sudden or unexpected death of your loved one is a devastating, painful event that can threaten the safety, stability, and security of your well-being, and your body automatically responds in a manner designed to protect you.

It is outside of the scope of this workbook to delve in detail into the body's response to trauma. You may have learned about the *fight, flight, or freeze response*, a complex physiological mechanism your body uses to cope with stressful or traumatic events. Your sympathetic nervous system was designed to activate your flight, fight, or freeze response so you can "outrun" or survive the stressor. Once the threat is resolved, your parasympathetic nervous system is supposed to signal your body to calm and restore itself to a relaxed state. Often, after the traumatic death of a loved one, the sympathetic nervous system remains activated. When this happens, your body is unable to return your nervous system to baseline, and you may begin to experience trauma symptoms.

The Trauma Response

The trauma response can be described as a normal response to an abnormal situation. A traumatic event can dramatically influence how you experience the world and impact everything; overnight, your entire life can change and become unrecognizable after the death of your loved one. Emotions can become difficult to control, causing you to feel untethered, feel lost, and or question your identity. After a traumatic event, some people do not report any trauma symptoms, or experience only minor symptoms that quickly diminish, whereas others experience symptoms that interfere with all aspects of functioning.

Trauma symptoms are complex and multidimensional, potentially surfacing immediately after a traumatic event or becoming problematic at a later time. Traumatic grief can impact how you think and feel, your interactions and relationships, and your ability to feel connected to your body or others. Trauma symptoms, your grief, and the loss of the assumptive world can make it difficult to trust yourself and others, or to exist in your surroundings.

Not everyone who experiences a sudden or unexpected death will develop symptoms associated with traumatic grief. More importantly, the presence or absence of trauma symptoms does not represent the love or the relationship you had with your loved one. Trauma symptoms reflect how your body is uniquely processing and reacting to the loss of your loved one. Traumatic grief is not a medical diagnosis or a pathological condition. It is a way for you to understand your current experience and find resources, such as this workbook, specific to your needs.

In the following table are some of the most common symptoms associated with traumatic grief. Please note this is not an exhaustive list of symptoms you may be experiencing or that may be possible.

Circle any words that describe your current symptoms and put an X through symptoms that you have previously encountered but no longer or rarely experience.

Physical	Emotional	Behavioral	Cognitive	Social
Headaches	Fear	Withdrawal or isolation	Trouble concentrating	Lack of interest in activities previously enjoyed
Stomachaches	Anxiety or panic	Compulsive behaviors	Memory loss	Feeling detached
Body aches	Easily startled or scared	High-risk behaviors	Confusion	Difficulty with relationships
Nausea	Changes in mood	Substance use (alcohol or drugs)	Distraction	
Trouble sleeping	Helplessness	Avoiding people, places, or things	Difficulty tracking time	
Appetite changes	Hopelessness		Slower thinking	
Fatigue	Numbness or detachment		Forgetfulness	
Weakness	Flashbacks			
Pounding heartbeat	Rumination			
	Intrusive memories			
	Nightmares			

I encourage you to return to this list periodically. In time, you will likely put an X over many of the symptoms that you have circled.

It is difficult to predict how you will respond to your loved one's death. Physically, you may not feel well. Traumatic grief can exacerbate any previous or existing health problems. I strongly encourage a medical checkup to rule out physical conditions that may be masked as symptoms of traumatic grief. Emotional reactions to a trauma often feel immense and can be initially difficult to regulate or control. One of the biggest challenges with a trauma is your previous coping mechanisms may not be sufficient to manage the distress at hand, leaving you with insufficient resources to cope.

Trauma also messes with the way you think. It can be very difficult to feel grounded and in control of your thought processes when your thinking is fuzzy, or you lack trust in your decision-making skills. I have had clients neglect to pay mortgages, not remember to change clocks after daylight savings, drive the wrong way on a one-way street adjacent to their home, or forget to pick up their children from school. One client described her headspace as "trying to wallpaper fog."

Trauma can also change your behaviors. This might make you unrecognizable to yourself, family, or friends, especially if you behave in a manner that is completely different from before your loved one's death.

Assessing Your Traumatic Grief Symptoms

The following worksheet will help you assess, track, and monitor the intensity and frequency of any current traumatic symptoms and how they progress as you proceed through this workbook. You can also download a copy at http://www.newharbinger.com/54926 and complete it as many times as is helpful. (Note: This exercise does not focus on grief symptoms and is not meant to diagnose clinical disorders associated with trauma.)

For each trauma symptom listed, circle the number that represents the corresponding intensity and frequency of the symptom.

Today's Date _____ **Date of Loved One's Death** _____

Symptom of Trauma The list below is not an exhaustive list of trauma symptoms. Please add any additional signs of trauma you are currently experiencing.	Intensity of Symptom None = 1 Minimal = 2 Slight = 3 Moderate = 4 Severe = 5	Frequency of Symptom Never = 1 Occasionally = 2 Intermittently = 3 Frequently = 4 Constantly = 5
Physical Symptoms		
Headaches	1 ... 2 ... 3 ... 4 ... 5	1 ... 2 ... 3 ... 4 ... 5
Stomachaches	1 ... 2 ... 3 ... 4 ... 5	1 ... 2 ... 3 ... 4 ... 5
Body aches	1 ... 2 ... 3 ... 4 ... 5	1 ... 2 ... 3 ... 4 ... 5
Nausea	1 ... 2 ... 3 ... 4 ... 5	1 ... 2 ... 3 ... 4 ... 5
Trouble sleeping	1 ... 2 ... 3 ... 4 ... 5	1 ... 2 ... 3 ... 4 ... 5
Appetite changes	1 ... 2 ... 3 ... 4 ... 5	1 ... 2 ... 3 ... 4 ... 5
Fatigue	1 ... 2 ... 3 ... 4 ... 5	1 ... 2 ... 3 ... 4 ... 5
Weakness	1 ... 2 ... 3 ... 4 ... 5	1 ... 2 ... 3 ... 4 ... 5
Pounding heartbeat	1 ... 2 ... 3 ... 4 ... 5	1 ... 2 ... 3 ... 4 ... 5
Other _____	1 ... 2 ... 3 ... 4 ... 5	1 ... 2 ... 3 ... 4 ... 5

Symptom of Trauma The list below is not an exhaustive list of trauma symptoms. Please add any additional signs of trauma you are currently experiencing.	Intensity of Symptom None = 1 Minimal = 2 Slight = 3 Moderate = 4 Severe = 5	Frequency of Symptom Never = 1 Occasionally = 2 Intermittently = 3 Frequently = 4 Constantly = 5
Emotional Symptoms		
Fear	1 ... 2 ... 3 ... 4 ... 5	1 ... 2 ... 3 ... 4 ... 5
Anxiety or panic	1 ... 2 ... 3 ... 4 ... 5	1 ... 2 ... 3 ... 4 ... 5
Easily startled or scared	1 ... 2 ... 3 ... 4 ... 5	1 ... 2 ... 3 ... 4 ... 5
Changes in mood	1 ... 2 ... 3 ... 4 ... 5	1 ... 2 ... 3 ... 4 ... 5
Helplessness	1 ... 2 ... 3 ... 4 ... 5	1 ... 2 ... 3 ... 4 ... 5
Hopelessness	1 ... 2 ... 3 ... 4 ... 5	1 ... 2 ... 3 ... 4 ... 5
Numbness or detachment	1 ... 2 ... 3 ... 4 ... 5	1 ... 2 ... 3 ... 4 ... 5
Flashbacks	1 ... 2 ... 3 ... 4 ... 5	1 ... 2 ... 3 ... 4 ... 5
Intrusive memories	1 ... 2 ... 3 ... 4 ... 5	1 ... 2 ... 3 ... 4 ... 5
Rumination	1 ... 2 ... 3 ... 4 ... 5	1 ... 2 ... 3 ... 4 ... 5
Nightmares	1 ... 2 ... 3 ... 4 ... 5	1 ... 2 ... 3 ... 4 ... 5
Other _____	1 ... 2 ... 3 ... 4 ... 5	1 ... 2 ... 3 ... 4 ... 5
Behavioral Symptoms		
Withdrawal or isolation	1 ... 2 ... 3 ... 4 ... 5	1 ... 2 ... 3 ... 4 ... 5
Compulsive behaviors	1 ... 2 ... 3 ... 4 ... 5	1 ... 2 ... 3 ... 4 ... 5
High-risk behaviors	1 ... 2 ... 3 ... 4 ... 5	1 ... 2 ... 3 ... 4 ... 5
Substance use (alcohol or drugs)	1 ... 2 ... 3 ... 4 ... 5	1 ... 2 ... 3 ... 4 ... 5
Avoiding people, places, or things	1 ... 2 ... 3 ... 4 ... 5	1 ... 2 ... 3 ... 4 ... 5
Other _____	1 ... 2 ... 3 ... 4 ... 5	1 ... 2 ... 3 ... 4 ... 5

Symptom of Trauma The list below is not an exhaustive list of trauma symptoms. Please add any additional signs of trauma you are currently experiencing.	Intensity of Symptom None = 1 Minimal = 2 Slight = 3 Moderate = 4 Severe = 5	Frequency of Symptom Never = 1 Occasionally = 2 Intermittently = 3 Frequently = 4 Constantly = 5
Cognitive Symptoms		
Trouble concentrating	1 ... 2 ... 3 ... 4 ... 5	1 ... 2 ... 3 ... 4 ... 5
Memory loss	1 ... 2 ... 3 ... 4 ... 5	1 ... 2 ... 3 ... 4 ... 5
Confusion	1 ... 2 ... 3 ... 4 ... 5	1 ... 2 ... 3 ... 4 ... 5
Distraction	1 ... 2 ... 3 ... 4 ... 5	1 ... 2 ... 3 ... 4 ... 5
Difficulty tracking time	1 ... 2 ... 3 ... 4 ... 5	1 ... 2 ... 3 ... 4 ... 5
Slower thinking	1 ... 2 ... 3 ... 4 ... 5	1 ... 2 ... 3 ... 4 ... 5
Forgetfulness	1 ... 2 ... 3 ... 4 ... 5	1 ... 2 ... 3 ... 4 ... 5
Other _____	1 ... 2 ... 3 ... 4 ... 5	1 ... 2 ... 3 ... 4 ... 5
Social Symptoms		
Lack of interest in activities previously enjoyed	1 ... 2 ... 3 ... 4 ... 5	1 ... 2 ... 3 ... 4 ... 5
Feeling detached	1 ... 2 ... 3 ... 4 ... 5	1 ... 2 ... 3 ... 4 ... 5
Difficulty with relationships	1 ... 2 ... 3 ... 4 ... 5	1 ... 2 ... 3 ... 4 ... 5
Other _____	1 ... 2 ... 3 ... 4 ... 5	1 ... 2 ... 3 ... 4 ... 5

Living with Trauma

Living with traumatic grief is often described as surreal and lonely. Clients frequently share how different they now feel, for example, no longer fitting in with others. You may feel like an outsider to family and friends who do not comprehend your new reality or take the time to understand your grief and pain. Intense, overwhelming emotions often increase your sensitivity to new stimulants in your environment. You may feel the need to hold constant vigilance, staying prepared for the next big thing, worrying about family and friends, or fearing for your own safety. Circumstances often make it easy to isolate, difficult to form relationships, trust others, ask for help, or seek support. Confusion, memory problems, distortion of time, or physical ailments may occur as you struggle with tasks and life responsibilities.

When your loved one has been abruptly taken from your life, it can feel like your foundation has been cracked, leaving you with a constant yearning for their presence and the life you previously created. At the same time, you may feel like a foreigner in your own body and the world in which you now reside. Despite this unimaginable grief, trauma, and pain, your body can survive and heal from this undesirable state.

The remainder of this chapter focuses on ways you can begin to manage and regulate your emotions and will help you establish safety in the immediate aftermath or through the intense periods of traumatic grief you will encounter throughout your healing experience.

Your Emotional Comfort Zone

Prior to your traumatic loss, your nervous system was able to ebb and flow with life's daily stressors in a comfortable manner. The boundary or space where your nervous system is healthy, balanced, and able to safely experience everyday highs and lows is what Daniel Siegel, MD, has defined as the *window of tolerance* and is shown in figure 1 (Siegel 2020).

A Healthy Nervous System

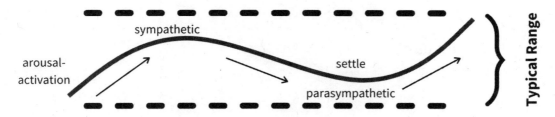

A healthy nervous system (Siegel 2020, produced with permission) stays in balance with typical ebbs and flows in response to an arousal, such as a stressor, within an optimal zone of arousal, called the window of tolerance. Your sympathetic nervous system activates your body to respond to an arousal. Your parasympathetic nervous system signals your body to settle and restore itself to a relaxed state once the arousal is resolved.

If the sudden or unexpected death of your loved one forced your nervous system outside of the optimal zone of arousal, you are most likely experiencing a state of hyperarousal, hypoarousal, or a combination of both as seen in Figure 2 (Siegel 2020). A state of *hyperarousal* is like the fight, flight, or freeze response.

Hyperarousal symptoms may include:

- Anxiety

- Panic

- Inability to relax

- Restlessness

- Emotional flooding

- Chronic pain

- Hypervigilance

- Trouble sleeping

- Irritability

Hypoarousal is a "flop" or "faint" reaction. Symptoms may include:

- Depression

- Exhaustion

- Chronic fatigue

- Disassociation

- Pain

- Disconnection

- Emotional numbness

- Feelings of emptiness

A Nervous System Outside of the Window of Tolerance

Hyperarousal Symptoms include:
- Anxiety
- Panic
- Inability to relax
- Restlessness
- Emotional flooding
- Chronic pain

Typical Range

Hypoarousal Symptoms include:
- Depression
- Exhaustion
- Chronic Fatigue
- Dissociation
- Pain
- Disconnection

A nervous system outside the window of tolerance (Siegel 2020, produced with permission) is characterized by arousal outside the typical range. Hyperarousal is above the typical range; hypoarousal is below the typical range.

The goal now is to regulate your emotions so you can find your window of tolerance and move back toward your optimal zone.

Tools to Help with Uncontrolled Emotions

There are simple techniques you can use to regulate your emotions during a trauma response or intense moments of grief. You may have even tried them before. If so, I invite you to try them again, with your new understanding of traumatic grief, the body's trauma response, and the window of tolerance. These tools are not one-size-fits-all. What works for someone may not work for someone else. Similarly, what has or has not worked for you before may work differently now. Practice each of the following tools when you are not experiencing intense trauma symptoms. This will provide you with a sense of comfort and skill. By using these techniques when you are not in a crisis, you will more easily recognize how to soothe yourself and regulate your emotions during moments of acute traumatic grief symptoms.

Deep Breathing

Your breath is a powerful instrument, and deep breathing is a formidable technique to counteract the shallow breathing that often occurs with the fight, flight, or freeze response.

BOX BREATHING

Box breathing, also known as square breathing or 4 x 4 breathing, involves slow, deep breaths in a simple four-step process. Imagine tracing the four equal sides of a box or square as you complete each of the following steps:

- Breathe in slowly for the count of four.

- Hold your breath for the count of four.

- Exhale for the count of four.

- Hold your breath for the count of four.

Repeat this exercise as needed, until you feel calmer and can focus on something besides your emotions or feelings.

LONG EXHALES

Lengthening your exhales can help calm your body and can be extremely beneficial if you are hyperventilating.

- Start with a large exhale to empty your lungs.

- Inhale for a count of four.

- Exhale for a count of six to eight.

Repeat this cycle of breathing for three to five minutes or until your breathing begins to regulate.

Grounding Exercises

Grounding exercises help with emotional regulation by reorienting you to the here and now and away from distressing thoughts, emotions, or memories. My favorite grounding exercise uses your five senses. To begin, sit in a chair with your feet on the ground, gently close your eyes, and take some deep breaths. Then pay attention to each of your senses one at a time by doing the following:

- Name five things in the environment you saw around you that you remember when your eyes were open.

- List four sounds that you can hear.

- With your eyes still closed, describe three fragrances you can smell.

- Put your hands on your lap and describe two things you feel.

- Think about the last thing you tasted.

Continue with a series of deep breaths until your emotions start to feel calmer. You can get up and change rooms if you would like to repeat this exercise.

Additional grounding exercises include counting backward from twenty-five, reciting the alphabet backward, or engaging in any cognitive activity that requires you to think, which distracts your mind from reengaging emotionally with the trauma.

Changing Energy

There are two ways to change your energy: change the energy in your environment or change the energy in your body.

CHANGE THE ENERGY IN YOUR ENVIRONMENT

When you experience trauma, it is easy to isolate yourself or stay inside, and after a while, it is common to feel like the walls are closing in. To change energy in your environment, go somewhere else, preferably outdoors in nature or in the sunshine. Go for a drive, run an errand, or go to a coffee shop. Many times, when you are hurting, the environment you are living in is often hurting as well. You may not realize that staying inside or isolation can exacerbate emotions that feel difficult to control. When working with clients, I strongly encourage them to leave their house at least once a day not only to shift their energy but to also prevent an increase in grief or a depressed mood.

CHANGE THE ENERGY IN YOUR BODY

Gentle walking or other physical movement is also very effective with emotional regulation. Even small amounts of exercise can increase your endorphins, otherwise known as your feel-good chemicals. When you work your muscles, they can become fatigued, which often leaves you feeling more relaxed and accomplished, and improves your overall well-being. I have yet to hear anyone say I felt worse (emotionally) after engaging in movement. Walking, yoga, tai chi, and even stretching can change the energy in your body.

Frozen Object

When you start to experience intense emotions, especially a stress response due to anxiety, or feel yourself entering the fight, flight, or freeze response, you might find it helpful to use a frozen orange, or other piece of citrus, or a frozen water bottle to help regulate your emotions.

Place the fruit between your hands, take deep breaths, and just focus on it. Feel the cold, the texture, and the weight. Just sit there with it for as long as it feels comfortable or as needed. This technique may be beneficial because the frozen fruit acts as a distraction and gives you something to focus on rather than feelings, such as overwhelm. The cold may also act as a temporary reset for your nervous system. Most of my clients find this technique extremely helpful and report a decrease in their anxiety after holding the frozen item. When you are done with the exercise, don't forget to put your fruit back in the freezer, so it is ready if and when you need it again.

The best way to master the techniques presented is to practice each of them when you are not experiencing intense symptoms of emotional dysregulation. The following worksheet will help you make a care plan about how you can use the techniques during periods of intense grief.

Care Plan for Soothing Emotions in Traumatic Grief

In the following table, rate your overall feelings about how helpful each tool will be in calming or soothing intense emotions. Record any thoughts or feelings about your experiences while using each technique under the notes column. After you complete the table, list the top three techniques you plan to use to help calm your emotions during intense periods of traumatic grief. This will save you from having to decide what to do when you are struggling with intense emotions.

Tools for Emotional Regulation	Perceived Helpfulness 1 = not at helpful 5 = extremely helpful	Notes
Deep Breathing Box breathing Long exhales	 1 … 2 … 3 … 4 … 5 1 … 2 … 3 … 4 … 5	
Grounding Exercises Five senses Counting backward by 25 Reciting alphabet backward	 1 … 2 … 3 … 4 … 5 1 … 2 … 3 … 4 … 5 1 … 2 … 3 … 4 … 5	
Changing Energy In the environment In the body	 1 … 2 … 3 … 4 … 5 1 … 2 … 3 … 4 … 5	
Frozen Objects Frozen citrus Frozen water bottle	 1 … 2 … 3 … 4 … 5 1 … 2 … 3 … 4 … 5	

Based on my responses above, my care plan to use during periods of intense emotional dysregulation will be to use the following three techniques:

_____

_____

_____

Creating Safety and Comfort

After a traumatic event, it is common to view the world differently, with a new sensitivity toward safety or risk. When living with traumatic grief, creating safety is of primary importance; however, the meaning of the term will differ for everyone. In general, safety is being protected from harm, injury, or death. But it can be hard to feel safe when someone you loved was not safe and abruptly died.

In their book, *I Wasn't Ready to Say Goodbye*, authors Brook Noel and Pamela Blair, PhD, encourage readers to put themselves in a metaphorical emotional intensive care unit after the sudden death of a loved one for this very reason (Noel and Blair 2008). Currently, you may find safety in certain people, places, items, or belongings. You may feel safest being alone in your home or with others somewhere else. Safety, for you, may include certain smells, foods, temperatures, animals, or sounds. Safety may also include avoiding certain people, places, or things for the time being. Your definition of safety is personal and may quickly change or evolve over time. What matters most is that you create a sense of safety that has the potential to offer respite from your grief, an atmosphere to regulate your nervous system, and a space conducive to making decisions about your next steps.

Write your personal definition of safety:

_____

_____

Affirmations, or self-affirming statements, are another way to feel safe during difficult times. Sometimes, we need to remind or reassure ourselves that in the present moment, we are not in harm's way and are loved. Try repeating affirmations, such as "I am safe," "I am okay," or "I am loved," to yourself at times when you find yourself questioning your feelings of safety.

List three affirmations you can use when feeling unsafe:

_____

_____

_____

Creating Safety Exercise

The following exercise will help you identify people, places, and things you can bring into your life to enhance immediate safety and comfort. Your sense of safety may change or evolve over time. You can redo this exercise by downloading it at http://www.newharbinger.com/54926 and completing it as many times as is helpful.

Suggestions for Creating Safety	My Safety List
People who make me feel safe Examples: My best friend, my sibling	
Places where I feel safe Examples: At home, in the garden, at church	
Sounds, smells, or foods that feel safe Examples: Quiet music, candles, soup	
Objects that make me feel safe Examples: Soft blankets, my loved one's shirt, stuffed animal	
Other things that make me feel safe Examples: My dog or cat	
People, places, or things you want to avoid Examples: The car, being alone	

If you are struggling with creating safety and comfort, you may find it helpful to keep your affirmations and safety list in an easily accessible location so you can refer to them when needed. Enlist the support of those you feel comfortable with to help you establish an environment that will help feel at ease while grieving.

Concluding Thoughts

The body is amazingly resilient and able to process and work through traumatic events. It is important to give yourself the time and space to learn how to regulate your emotions to begin regaining a sense of control over them and establishing a sense of safety to support your healing process. Although the immediate aftermath of a traumatic death is overwhelming and intense, as each day passes, your body and mind are learning to acclimate and absorb your new circumstances. Investing in strengthening your initial foundation and resources prepares you to explore the grief you are feeling for your loved one.

In the next chapter, you will continue to build upon and expand your resources with more ways to create safety as well as mechanisms to reestablish a sense of normalcy.

CHAPTER 3

Emerge From Under the Covers to Find Support

There will come a time when you will be ready to metaphorically "climb out of bed" and actively start to reengage with your life. This might be within days of learning the news, or within weeks, months, or even longer. The amount of time does not matter. The signal will come from within, as a yearning for your life to return to "normal," the way it used to be when your loved one was alive. When your life was not turned upside down, your emotions were not a disheveled mess, and things just made sense. This chapter builds on the tools you learned in chapter 2 to expand your ability to feel safe so that you can begin to create your new normal, starting with routine and structure.

Some of the things I hear most often from clients include, "I just want my life to go back to the way it was" or "I just want things to be normal again." I'm sure you've figured out by now that your life is not returning to the old normal you once knew. Unfortunately, not only has your loved one died, but you also probably feel a part of you died with them, and you are no longer the same person you were before. The trauma has changed everything.

Your yearning for things to be normal is partly connected to your desire to feel safe again. You want to feel okay again, for your life to return to the way it was, and for all to be right with your world. While your loved one will not return, the feelings you long for can. You can feel safe again. You can feel okay again. And someday, you will experience happiness, joy, or peace again.

So how do you learn to live with shattered assumptions, new life circumstances, the emotional pain, trauma, and symptoms that come with the sudden or unexpected death of someone you love? You begin by creating a new normal. You start by consciously and intentionally constructing a safe space, finding a set of practices, and surrounding yourself with a supportive group of people to walk alongside you as you slowly begin to move toward healing. Starting over is not easy or may not seem like it's worth the effort, but I invite you to have an open mind as we walk through the chapter exercises and skills together.

Routine and Structure

One of the first things I encourage you to assess, regardless of the amount of time that has elapsed since your loss, is your daily routine. Your daily routine provides you with a framework of tasks, responsibilities, and self-care activities that build in structure, purpose, and even distractions necessary to manage and live with traumatic grief. Research has shown that routines and daily structure also have a positive impact on mental health, increase productivity, and encourage momentum (Heintzelman and King 2019).

While you are living with traumatic grief, a daily routine and structure will provide a sense of control when life seems out of control and chaotic. Performing and repeating the same group of activities reestablishes a sense of predictability, order, and safety in your life. With a dependable routine, your new normal will slowly begin to emerge. Your body will learn it is okay to begin to trust again. Your emotions will have a better chance to regulate, especially if you include activities such as mindfulness or other forms of restorative self-care that will help you be present in your daily life.

Before thinking about the routine you would like to create, consider what your days look like right now. If you have returned to work or are caring for someone else, there may already be significant structure in your days. In that case, when reviewing how your current time is structured, I encourage you to think about the times outside of your work or caregiving activities. Consider the following questions:

How am I spending most of my time right now?

_____

_____

_____

_____

_____

_____

What parts or times of my day are the hardest? The easiest? Why?

_____

_____

_____

_____

_____

How can I design my day to protect myself and provide extra comfort when I struggle the most?

_____

_____

_____

_____

_____

When you are living with traumatic grief, here are some ways to help you build a routine that will work for you.

- Create something realistic.

- Tailor your routine to support you during the times of the day that are most challenging. For example, if the evenings are the hardest time of your day, make sure your routine includes a supportive activity at night to help you cope.

- Allow for flexibility and give yourself grace when you find yourself overwhelmed with intense feelings of trauma or grief and need a break from structure.

- Include self-care in your routine to help you experience respite from your grief and trauma.

Use the space in the table to record how you currently spend your days and to identify the routine you would like to create.

	Current Routine		Ideal Routine	
	Weekdays	Weekend	Weekdays	Weekend
Wake Time				
Morning Activities				
Lunch				
Afternoon Activities				
Dinner				
Evening Activities				
Bedtime				

Self-Care

Let's talk about self-care in more detail. The concept of self-care takes on a different meaning when you are living with traumatic grief. It is a necessity for survival and essential to function and cope so your body and mind can begin to calm, regulate, and heal. Traumatic grief drains your energy and makes it difficult to attend to life's responsibilities. Self-care can be any healthy activity you engage in on a regular, consistent basis that maintains your ability to function and contributes to your sense of restoration. It is an opportunity to replenish the emotional and physical energy that is constantly being depleted.

As you know, you do not grieve in a bubble. Not only are you coping with emotional pain and trauma symptoms, but you also still have responsibilities at work or home and may have others who are dependent on you to have their needs met. Unless you care for yourself, there is no way you will be able to care for others. When you are grieving, you will benefit from a comprehensive self-care plan that addresses your physical, emotional, intellectual, social, spiritual, and grief needs. Self-care can be a distraction to give your mind and body a time-out from the intensity of pain you experience on a day-to-day basis, and sometimes, self-care is an intentional deep dive to process your traumatic grief. The following list includes activities that may help you meet your self-care needs.

- **Physical:** going to the doctor, eating a nutritious diet, exercising, and sleeping

- **Emotional:** journaling, dancing, engaging in creative pursuits, singing, and spending time with animals

- **Intellectual:** reading, doing puzzles, listening to podcasts, and taking classes

- **Social:** having deep and meaningful social interactions, including time with family or friends, social activities, and supportive digital communication, such as texts and emails

- **Spiritual:** practicing meditation, spending time in nature, volunteering, or connecting with a higher being

- **Grief:** visiting the cemetery, reminiscing, talking to a therapist, and attending support groups

There are parts of self-care that are not as alluring as curling up in bed and reading a good book. Self-care also includes saying no and setting limits with yourself and others. When you are grieving, an important part of self-care is about setting boundaries. This means protecting your energy and space. It is also about setting limits to honor your needs and giving yourself permission to avoid interactions that will further drain you or are not in the best interest of your healing.

Self-care can also involve giving yourself a gentle push to engage in activities that will be beneficial, even if you feel that they require too much energy. This can include activities like getting out of bed, attending a social activity with supportive friends, or even limiting unhealthy behaviors to numb the pain. It can be hard to set limits with yourself and others when you are hurting. Learn how to check in with yourself before making commitments to yourself and others. Setting limits is never easy; however, these boundaries will help with your healing.

You may intellectually realize the benefits of self-care but struggle to make these activities part of a daily routine. It is easy to believe that self-care is not possible when you are grieving and that you do not have the bandwidth to engage. However, committing to self-care is a fundamental part of your grieving process. I invite you to begin thinking daily about what you need to care for yourself. Nothing is going to take away your traumatic grief, but there are ways to slowly decrease the intensity of your pain, bit by bit.

The following exercise has space for you to generate a list of self-care activities that will help meet your needs. Next to each activity, there is room to write about expected feelings and outcomes you might experience after participating in each activity. This information can be beneficial in helping you select the best self-care options to fulfill specific needs.

Self-Care Dimension	Self-Care Activities	Expected Feelings and Outcomes
Physical	Example: Walk three times per week	Example: Won't like it at first, be glad I did it
Emotional	Example: Journal	Example: Mixture of emotions, relieved to express them
Intellectual	Example: Listen to mystery podcast	Example: Distracted in a good way, nice to have a grief break
Social	Example: Go to weekly poker game	Example: Disconnected from friends at first, less disconnected after
Spiritual	Example: Meditate	Example: Hard to be still, feel calmer
Grief	Example: Visit cemetery	Example: Sad, feel more connected

Like routine and structure, self-care takes planning and commitment. It may feel foreign at first, but I encourage you to continue and to modify your self-care plan as you receive insight and feedback from within. Over time, I believe you will find the right activities that will help your body and mind settle into a calmer state of being that is restorative and healing. Friends and family can be a major part of your self-care and healing from traumatic grief. The final section of this chapter explores relationship dynamics within your support system while you are grieving.

Relationships with Family and Friends

Part of coming out from under the covers includes reconnecting with family, friends, and others outside of your immediate circle who have been supporting you on a daily basis. You may have noticed that people you never expected have shown up to support you, while those you predicted would be available may have disappointed you. Be open to the change in your relationships, but don't give up on those who truly care about you. Help them help you. This is new territory for everybody.

Despite your desire to reengage, it is common to feel disconnected from others, encounter social interactions where your traumatic grief is not acknowledged, or even feel pressured to act as if everything is "just fine." Surrounding yourself with a supportive network is vital to creating a new normal and feeling safe. Yet, finding the right people to walk alongside you is easier said than done. You need a supportive group to validate your experiences and pain, who understand the long-term impact of your trauma and are committed to being a companion with you as you are healing. Along the way, I encourage you to be open to meeting and inviting new friends to be part of your story.

After your loved one's death, many of your family and friends do not know how to relate or react, or they may be fearful of saying the wrong things, so they don't say anything at all or they just disappear. This may leave you feeling even more isolated, traumatized, and without support at the time when you need it the most. You probably get the customary but cursory "How are you?" I have had too many clients share the heartache of being with friends who do not ask "How are you really doing?" or "What it is this like for you?" Perhaps, even worse is participating in a social interaction and, after spending several hours with others, noticing that your loved one was never mentioned. You're likely saddened that the elephant in the room was not acknowledged or feel that your loved one has been forgotten.

Unfortunately, it is also all too common to have family and friends say inappropriate or judgmental comments when you are grieving, which can be extremely hurtful. Many people have shared with me that their loved one was blamed for their death because they were a smoker, overweight, used drugs, rode a motorcycle, or decided to end their lives by suicide. I have worked with people who have been the recipient of remarks related to the amount of time they are taking to grieve when friends say unhelpful things like "It has already been a year, you should be over that by now." Others have had their losses invalidated by comments such as "Well, at least you didn't lose a child, that hurts even more." Others have had to bear insults such as "You are young; you can always have another child." And finally there are comments with religious undertones, including "You should feel good knowing they are with God now." When friends, family, colleagues, or even people outside of your immediate circle make judgments about your loved one's role in their death, engage in competitive grief, attempt to minimize your loss, comment about the duration of your grief, or use religion to comfort you, try and remind yourself that these comments are really about them and their discomfort with how to help or cope with grief.

I do believe that there are people in your life who want to help you but do not know what to say, what you need, or how to best support you in your traumatic grief. They are probably unaware that you are always thinking about what happened and that it's okay for them to initiate a discussion about your loved one. They may also be unaware that you enjoy talking about your loved one because it keeps them alive. These are the friends worth investing in—friends who would benefit from knowing how you feel and what you need. So many people want to help but do not know what to do. I encourage you to provide specific examples, such as "Could you go for a walk with me, run errands, pick up the kids, take my mom to the doctor, teach me a craft, or go to dinner and not talk about grief (or talk about grief)." You will be more likely to get the support you need if you share with friends and family: "I am always thinking about them, talking about them allows me to continuously express my love, or I like it when you ask about them." Don't be afraid to say "it hurts my feelings when you don't bring them up." or "Please don't say this…because it makes me feel this way…"

The following questions will help you reflect on the interactions you have had with family and friends throughout your grieving experiences. Use the information to strengthen communication between you and your support network and to move forward in your growth and healing process.

Reflect on a time when you felt supported in your grief by family or friends. What happened or what was said in that interaction to make you feel cared for?

_____

_____

_____

_____

Think about a time when you did not feel supported in your grief by friends or family. What happened or what was said in that interaction that did not make you feel cared for?

_____

_____

_____

_____

When it comes to your traumatic loss, what do you need from family or friends? How do you want to be treated?

_____

_____

_____

_____

How can you guide your friends or family to provide the support you need in your grief?

_____

_____

_____

_____

What topics or activities do you want your friends or family to avoid?

_____

_____

_____

_____

_____

What do you want your friends or family to say or talk about?

_____

_____

_____

_____

_____

What other actions do you want from your friends or family?

_____

_____

_____

_____

_____

If you are not able to get the support you need from family and friends, don't be afraid to expand your support circle to mental health professionals, support groups, clergy, or other individuals in different areas of your life. The most important thing is that you find people who can validate and witness your story and pain and reassure you that what you are experiencing is a natural part of grief.

Concluding Thoughts

Coming out from under the covers is a major step in reengaging with the world after the sudden or unexpected death of your loved one. It is important to take the time you need to reenter your world feeling safe, stable, and supported. A new normal is not created overnight. Instead, it is sculpted slowly through trial and error. Despite your vast pain and trauma, focus on the parts of the process that you can control. You get to decide the safe and supportive people you want to surround yourself with at this time. You get to choose self-care that is restorative and nourishing to meet your needs, and you get to create a structure (outside of predetermined work or caregiving responsibilities) to enhance your well-being and ability to function at the highest level given the constraints of your traumatic grief. Trust yourself and the protective voice within.

Chapters 1–3 offer foundational information and practical tools to help you start stabilizing and building resources after the traumatic death of your loved one. It is important not to rush this process. Take the time you need to create safety and learn to regulate your emotions. In time, your body and emotions will begin to feel safe again, and your trauma symptoms should begin to decrease in intensity.

In the next chapter, you will begin to transition your focus from your trauma to grieving the loss of your loved one.

CHAPTER 4

Recall Your Loved One Beyond How They Died

Beneath the story and trauma of how your loved one died is a mountain of raw grief. Now that you have created a safety plan and are better able to calm and regulate your nervous system, you are in a stronger place to address the enormous hole created by the unforeseen departure of your loved one. This chapter focuses on pure grief and delves deeper into the complexities of grieving your sudden or unexpected loss. We will look at the differences between primary and secondary losses and future and present losses. You will learn techniques to help you mourn and adapt to what is no longer.

You will acknowledge and celebrate your loved one for the beauty of their being, in absence of their trauma, to begin minimizing the impact the traumatic events have on you and the story of your loved one's life. Finally, you will explore the intended outcomes of grief work, so that you can begin to incorporate activities of your choice into your routine that integrate your loved one's essence as you continue to move toward healing.

As you know, death, loss, and grief are universal experiences everyone encounters during their lifespan. Some of us and the people we love will grow old and die of natural causes, while others will die early and unexpectedly. Although your individual circumstances differ from those of others, no one escapes the pain of grief. To love and grieve is to be human, and the emotions and sorrow that accompany grief are a core part of the person you are today. Your previous losses and trauma influence how you are adapting. Even without trauma, grief is more complicated when it occurs outside the expected order of the lifecycle. Parents never expect to bury their children, the sick do not expect to outlive the healthy, and there continues to be constant shock and horror in the random events that claim innocent lives.

As you begin to focus on your grief, you will notice a range and combination of feelings while mourning the death of your loved one. Despite your individual circumstances, there are common emotional experiences consistent with grief including:

- **Sadness:** a profound or overwhelming feeling of sadness, sorrow, or pain stemming from the absence of your loved one

- **Separation distress:** yearning and longing for your loved one and your relationship

- **Numbness:** feeling disconnected or numb to your life circumstances after the death of your loved one until you can better comprehend the enormity of your loss, often followed by intensified emotions

- **Denial:** an inability to accept the emotional reality of your loved one's death

- **Anger:** feeling angry at yourself, your loved one, others, a higher power, or the world at large for specific behaviors, actions, or the general unfairness of the situation

- **Anxiety:** fears about your future, stressors to living without your loved one, and concerns about the uncertainties in life

- **Loneliness:** withdrawal from social networks and increased disconnection from others

- **Memory loss:** confusion or memory loss due to emotional overwhelm, pain, and the effort to adapt to multiple changes in a short period of time, which can make you feel like you are losing your mind

Your grief experience is complex. In addition to the common grief emotions listed above, you most likely will contend with additional emotionally laden issues, including guilt, regret, self-blame, and a sudden loss of identity. These topics will be explored in-depth in later chapters. With or without symptoms of trauma, the sudden or unexpected death of your loved one has complicated your grieving process with the personal challenges and intense psychological issues you have been left to carry. It is important to remember that your grief experience will be different from others' and that your current loss will also differ from any previous deaths you have grieved earlier in your life. You may or may not experience all the emotions described above, but the emotions you do experience *will not be linear in nature* and will vary in intensity throughout your grieving process.

Primary and Secondary Losses

In death, grief is multidimensional in nature and usually comprises a primary loss and multiple secondary losses. The *primary loss* is your loved one who died. This is the root of your pain and the most obvious, tangible source of your grief. The abrupt absence of your loved one resulted in a cascade of physical, emotional, psychological, and practical consequences that are profound, and your initial energy is focused on meeting these needs.

Unfortunately, your loved one's death also initiated a series of additional losses connected to past traumas, present circumstances, and future dreams. *Secondary losses* are all the other losses directly related to the death of your loved one. These losses are like ripples in the water after you throw a stone. They are the consequences created from your primary loss, the death of your loved one. Secondary losses are broad and can include anything, including shifts in family dynamics, changes in your daily routine, fluctuations in your financial security, or a reevaluation of future plans. Secondary losses are often subtle and may not be immediately apparent, but they compound the complexity of grief by introducing more changes, often unwanted, in addition to the primary loss. For example, if you have experienced the death of a spouse, secondary losses may include the loss of a best friend, a travel companion, and a Sunday morning brunch buddy. And you may not realize until early April that you also lost your tax preparer.

I have many clients who describe secondary losses as harder to adapt to. They report missing, "the person I called on the way home from work," "the person who waited up for me when I got home at night," or "the only person who understood how difficult my boss really is." Secondary losses also include future losses. These losses can encompass: having a family of your own, watching a child graduate or raise their own family, or retiring and spending the rest of your life with someone you love. I remember one client saying, "They do not make condolence cards for secondary losses."

Identifying your secondary losses is a crucial part of working through your grief and is often a continual process happening over time. When you focus on your emotions beyond the death of your loved one, you will be better able to comprehend and communicate with those supporting you in grief. Secondary losses also provide insight about your grief that may be helpful later when you create a new grief narrative as part of your healing.

In the following columns, write examples of your secondary losses.

Present Losses	Future Losses
Examples: loss of walking partner, weekly phone calls	**Examples:** Growing old together, future travel adventures

Present Losses	Future Losses

Once you have identified your secondary losses, understanding what you need to grieve may not feel as overwhelming. Grieving the death of your spouse or partner, child, sibling, or friend can seem insurmountable. However, once you break down your grief and identify the secondary losses—such as your son's weekly calls or the retirement trip you were supposed to take with your spouse—it can make the process feel less overwhelming than trying to grieve the entire relationship at once. Either way, the hurt related to the absence of your loved one is incredibly painful, but the more detailed you can be in describing your loss, the easier it will be to begin working through the associated pain and grief.

Ways to Grieve Secondary Losses

Grieving your secondary losses is an important part of moving toward healing. Specific tasks or activities to focus on may help. Sometimes just the act of acknowledging your loss on paper will release some of the pain, but more often than not, it will take a combination of activities, such as sitting with your feelings, talking with others, writing, or engaging in a creative activity, to work through the complex emotions and pain embedded in a secondary loss. The following is a partial list of suggestions you can draw from to grieve your secondary losses:

- **Acknowledgement and validation:** The pain from secondary losses is real and intense. You took the first step by writing some of your losses above. Allow yourself to feel and express the full range of emotions that comes with secondary losses, including sadness, anger, or guilt.

- **Writing, journaling, or voice dictation:** An important part of working through your secondary losses is to get your thoughts and feelings out, instead of keeping them bottled up where they can consume you. Expressing your thoughts and emotions privately using paper, a computer, or an audio recording device releases them from inside. Recording them gives you an opportunity to track your progress and see how your internal dialogue changes over time.

- **Art projects:** Some people prefer a visual medium, such as collage, as a way to creatively express their feelings and pain. Creating art that represents your experiences can be a cathartic method to process the grief connected to your secondary losses.

- **Rituals and ceremonies:** Engaging in rituals or ceremonies that hold symbolic meanings to honor or mourn your secondary losses can be powerful ways to acknowledge endings and prepare for new beginnings.

- **Mindfulness activities:** Developing a mindfulness practice that includes practices such as meditation, yoga, gratitude, or moments of stillness can be extremely beneficial when the intensity of secondary losses feels overwhelming, and you need tools to help you feel grounded, calm, and present.

- **Join a support group:** Grief support groups provide a community of others also grieving secondary losses who can validate, empathize, and support you as you process and grieve your secondary losses.

A substantial amount of time I spend with clients in therapy is devoted to processing and grieving secondary losses. I have been privileged to witness clients express their pain in letters that have been read at the grave site, burned, or sent out to sea. I have seen clients create grief boxes, beautiful displays of loved one's personal mementos, and been awestruck by the beauty of artistic endeavors inspired by raw pain. I have been deeply moved by the individual ways grief can be expressed. Behind every memorial, ritual, and goodbye ceremony created in grief and pain connected to a secondary loss is an expression of enduring love and a bond that cannot be broken. There is no right or wrong way to grieve a secondary loss. The method you choose will be as distinct as your loved one, the nature of your relationship, and the time you spent together.

Reflect on your list of secondary losses. Start with one or two of the losses (present or future) causing you significant distress and use the space below to capture ideas or plans you can use to actively grieve or express your feelings to begin working through your pain.

_____

_____

_____

_____

_____

_____

_____

Processing secondary losses is a lengthy but vital part of your grief. Go slowly and pace yourself. Remember, grief is not linear, and do not get discouraged if you begin to feel a sense of release in one area and the grief reappears again later. I encourage you to honor your journey by allowing yourself to fully experience, without judgment, the wide range of thoughts and emotions that arise to celebrate the life of your loved one and the times you spent together.

Grieving Your Loved One and Not How They Died

It can be so easy to be consumed with how your loved one died. The pain you are experiencing and the circumstances surrounding the event can be all encompassing. However, the moment your loved one died represents only a small fraction of their life, just like the moment they were born and entered this world. Of importance is how they lived and their choices and actions while living. Celebrate their existence. Even though it may be difficult right now, remember and commemorate your loved one for who they were, rather than the way they died. When you cherish their memories based on the depth of their character, the warmth of their laughter, and the time you spent together, you will embrace what truly matters and the circumstances of their death will diminish in importance.

When you are in pain, it can be difficult or bittersweet to reminisce or celebrate a life that is no more. Similarly, it can be hard to feel grateful for the time you spent with your loved one who was abruptly taken from you. Remembering the unique qualities that defined your loved one, including their life story, attributes, achievements, and the legacy they left behind, rather than what you have lost and how the loss occurred will facilitate healing. The more you are able to focus on the memories, adventures, triumphs, and even struggles you shared with your loved one, the greater your likelihood will be to stay connected to the spirit and positive impact they brought to your life.

Use the space below to introduce your loved one to someone who did not have the opportunity to meet them. Describe their personality, values, passions, and interests. How would you sum up their life story? What was the footprint they left on the world, and how are you changed because of them? You may need extra space or paper for this exercise.

_____

_____

_____

_____

_____

_____

_____

Having the opportunity to talk, write, or share about your loved one, in absence of how they died, will help you stay connected to their positive attributes that often become temporarily overshadowed after a traumatic death.

Your Grief Diary

As you progress through the workbook and begin more formal grief work, I strongly encourage you start a grief diary or journal and aim to write in it daily, or as often as possible. Some people love to document, track, or express their thoughts and feelings in writing, whereas others shudder at the mere thought of such an activity. Journal writing is a very personal decision; however, the clients I have worked with who have committed to a daily grief journal have benefited greatly. Maintaining a grief journal will provide:

- A record of your grief and trauma symptoms that you can track over time

- Information to determine if new tools impact how you feel or reduce your symptoms

- An opportunity to understand the overarching patterns and themes in your grief

- Data about the functional impairment traumatic grief has on your life

- A container to express your emotions

- A place to celebrate accomplishments and achievements in your grief

- A comprehensive account of your grief trajectory to serve as a reminder of the progress you are making

Regular journaling means different things to different people. When you are overwhelmed with pain and grief, I know how hard it can be to commit to one more thing, especially as part of your daily routine. I encourage you to think of a grief journal as an investment in moving toward healing from your traumatic grief and an opportunity to learn from your grieving experience. I invite you to keep an open mind and give journaling a try. You can use a bullet journal format with short phrases or bullet points rather than write full sentences to make the process less daunting and time-consuming.

Daily Grief Journal

Here is a daily journal template designed to help you document and track your traumatic grief over 24 hours. I encourage you to download this page from http://www.newharbinger.com/54926 and complete this form daily.

Date _____ **Time of day** _____**am/pm**

Today…

I would describe my grief and emotional experiences (for example, sadness, numbness, anger) as:

_____

_____

I would describe my trauma symptoms (for example, hypervigilance, rumination, flashbacks, nightmares) as:

_____

_____

My physical sensations related to my traumatic grief (for example, pain, tension, fatigue) were:

_____

_____

My sleep can best be described as:

_____

_____

I estimate the total number of hours I slept last night was _____.

The following number best represents how intense my traumatic grief felt.

1	2	3	4	5	6	7	8	9	10

Not at all intense   *Extremely intense*

The following number best represents how well I coped with my traumatic grief.

1	2	3	4	5	6	7	8	9	10

Not at all well   *Extremely well*

I had the following memories of my loved one who died:

_____

_____

I want to record or process the following experiences related to my traumatic grief (for example, events, conversations, activities):

_____

_____

I engaged in the following self-care activities (for example, exercise, mindfulness, time with friends):

_____

_____

I thought about the following unanswered questions or uncertainties related to my loved one:

_____

_____

I had the following positive thoughts or feelings of gratitude:

_____

_____

I reflected on the following changes about my traumatic grief:

_____

_____

_____

_____

I want to record the following observations and thoughts to remember about my grief:

_____

_____

_____

_____

_____

I believe you will find your grief diary a helpful tool. The information you collect can guide you in making adjustments in how you respond to your grief and remind you of topics, questions, and memories you want to explore as you continue healing.

Concluding Thoughts

Grief work is laborious and hard. Use the information you learned in this chapter to serve as guideposts for your grief and pain, particularly as you deal with both primary and secondary losses, as well as present and future losses.

When you are in the midst of overwhelming emotions and a sea of losses, it can be easy to feel like your pain will never end. The tools in this chapter can serve as a map to remind you that a way through your pain exists. Feeling and expressing the difficult emotions and grieving the losses that present themselves after the death of your loved one are necessary experiences that will move you toward integration and healing. Look for ways to honor, celebrate, and focus on the essence of your loved one, in absence of the manner of their death, so you can lay the foundation for continued bonds yet to come.

In the next chapter, we will focus on new ways to live with your traumatic grief on a daily basis, so it does not feel like a full-time job.

CHAPTER 5

Ways to Manage Grief So It's Not a Full-Time Job

Living with traumatic grief can feel like a full-time job. You may feel your world lacks color or that your days are long, devoid of meaning, or without direction. After a hard day of grief work, it is important to remember that you need a break. You are not meant to live your life in constant pain. Even though the death of your loved one brought unwanted disruption and grief into your life, sooner or later, your traumatic grief will settle and become part of your daily cadence.

This chapter delves deeper into different ways you can learn to tolerate your traumatic grief and integrate grief breaks and restorative activities into your daily routine. You will also have a chance to solidify and practice the skills you learned in previous chapters, so you can function at the highest level possible alongside the grief and trauma symptoms you continue to experience.

Dual Process Model of Coping with Bereavement

Over the years, many theoretical models have been developed to understand the grieving experience and guide grievers through the overwhelming emotions, stressors, and problems associated with loss. One of my favorite models to illustrate this process is the dual process model of coping with bereavement developed by Margaret Stroebe, PhD, and Henk Schut, PhD, as shown in figure 3. According to the dual process model, you cope with your loved one's death by oscillating between two categories of coping: loss-oriented and restorative-oriented coping.

Loss-oriented coping is your active grief work. When you are in loss-orientated coping, you are engaged in activities such as processing the death of your loved one, yearning for their presence, crying, thinking about the circumstances of their death, pining for your life that used to be, or mourning the secondary losses no longer available as options. Loss-oriented coping is primarily focused on the past and working through your pain and grief.

Restoration-orientated coping, on the other hand, is mostly future focused and includes distractions from grief and adapting to your new life changes. While in restorative-oriented coping, you are focused on taking time out from your grief, although it still often lurks in the back of your mind. These activities can include sleeping, spending time with friends, zoning out on technology, or engaging in other actions that allow you to disconnect. Although the restoration-oriented activities are not grief work, the focus on future activities, such as learning how to live without your loved one, developing new routines and skills, and starting to rebuild your life, can be stressful experiences.

The premise of this model is that you are continually moving back and forth between these two forms of coping. Early on, you will spend more time in the loss-oriented activities, but as you continue to move toward healing, you will lean into more restorative activities that address secondary losses, such as changes in your identity, loneliness, and adaptation to new roles.

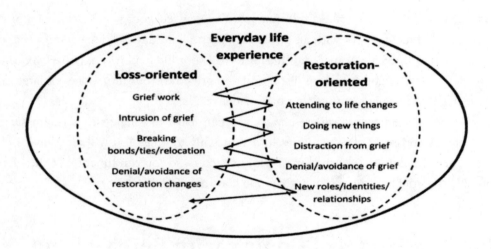

In the dual process model of coping with bereavement, you cope with your loved one's death by oscillating between two categories of coping, loss-oriented and restorative-oriented, in your everyday life (Stroebe and Schut 1999, reproduced with permission).

The oscillation dynamic between the loss and restoration perspectives may be different after the traumatic or violent death of your loved one. Edward Rynearson, MD, adapted the model by Stroebe and Schut and created the dual process model of bereavement in the context of a violent death. His version of the model includes how a violent death (for example, suicide, accident, or homicide) can overshadow the loss orientation when there are symptoms of traumatic distress, invasive reenactments of your loved one dying, or existential despair (Rynearson 2012).

I invite you to think about your current ways of coping with the death of your loved one. Using the framework outlined by the dual process model, write down some of your loss and restoration-oriented ways of coping.

Loss-oriented coping

Examples: Talking about your loved one, going to therapy, sitting with uncomfortable feelings

_____

_____

_____

_____

_____

_____

Restoration-oriented coping

Examples: Watching a movie, gardening, spending time with friends, making future plans

_____

_____

_____

_____

_____

_____

Tools for Pacing Yourself in Grief

The dual process model introduces the notion that you do not grieve twenty-four hours a day, seven days a week. There are times when you just need a break. You need to distract yourself from the intensity of the pain you are feeling. Grief is a long-term expedition and not a short journey. It is like running a long-term race or even an ultramarathon. It is not a sprint. Regular, consistent grief work (like preparing for a marathon) means pacing yourself with a realistic cadence, patience, grit, and perseverance. Although there is no finish line, there is a meaningful future ahead. Let's explore two closely related tools I use with clients learning to live with the daily rhythm of traumatic grief: a grief break and pleasant event scheduling.

Grief Break

The first tool for pacing yourself in grief is the all-important grief break, or grief time-out. Some of these activities fall within the restoration-oriented category of coping, illustrated in figure 3. You are used to taking a break or giving yourself a short period of rest from nearly everything you do in life, including work, school, exercise, chores, and relationships. Why should grief be any different? Research has shown that when we take breaks from our daily tasks, we experience an improvement in mood, reduced stress, changes in energy, and increased overall well-being (Korpela et al. 2016).

The same can be said for grief. When you give yourself a pause from experiencing the intensity of your grief, you may also experience shifts in your energy, mood, and clarity. Thus, you are able to reassess or reflect on your loved one and grief in a new way. Taking an intentional grief break is essential to pacing yourself and ensuring that you are not in constant pain.

Pleasant Event Scheduling

The second tool for pacing yourself in grief, *pleasant event scheduling*, helps you implement your grief time-outs. Studies have demonstrated the importance of incorporating pleasant events into your daily life for overall well-being (Lewinsohn and Libet 1972). When you are grieving, engaging in pleasant events can generate positive emotions and feelings of contentment, reduce stress or worry, and divert your thoughts away from your grief. As such, work on scheduling pleasant events on a daily, weekly, and monthly or quarterly basis, with events increasing in magnitude over time. When you make the time to do something enjoyable each day, such as watch a favorite television show, enjoy a meal, or meet with a friend, you have something to look forward to even when living in a continued state of intense grief.

Scheduling an outing, a day trip, or an experience each week adds anticipation. Having a vacation or trip to see family or friends on the horizon every few months also provides something positive to await.

Studies have shown that neural changes in the brain can accompany the ongoing release of dopamine, a neurotransmitter that enhances positive feelings and emotions, when anticipating something that is rewarding (Luo et al. 2018; Schultz 2016). Consistent pleasant event scheduling will help provide respite from your grief and may also improve your overall mood and general well-being.

Use the following space to identify pleasant events you can schedule and incorporate into your life on a daily, weekly, and monthly/quarterly basis.

Daily
Examples: Favorite food, TV show, phone call with friend

_____

_____

_____

_____

_____

Weekly
Examples: Museum, day trip, beach

_____

_____

_____

_____

_____

Monthly/Quarterly
Examples: Vacation, visit family or friends

_____

_____

_____

_____

_____

_____

Distractions

You may be wondering how it is possible to take a grief time-out or schedule pleasant events when you are in so much pain. Sometimes, it is just not. The grief is too painful and intense. If you find yourself in this situation, try choosing a distraction, or something that will temporarily divert you from your pain. You can use anything as a distraction that does not harm you. It can be meaningless television, a walk, a puzzle, time with pets or children, or a phone call with a friend.

One of the best distractions is doing something for another person in need or in pain. The purpose of a distraction is to participate in an activity that will briefly change your energy or mindset to give you a break or get you through an intense moment of grief. I once worked with a client who asked if his life was destined to be full of meaningless activities and distractions. I assured him that these diversions were an integral part of the early traumatic grief experience, and, over time, his distractions would slowly transition into meaningful activities he would anticipate and begin to enjoy. Today, although his grief still exists, he has rebuilt his life with meaningful relationships and experiences joy and pleasure in his daily activities. He also looks forward to the things he plans. Please do not feel disheartened if the thought of pleasurable activities does not resonate with you at this time. Focus on practicing grief time-outs and using distractions.

Write a list of distractions you can turn to when you cannot think of anything that sounds pleasant, such as helping others, doing puzzles, or walking the dog:

_____

_____

_____

_____

_____

_____

_____

Although you may not immediately detect changes in your mood or decreases in your grief and pain, with consistent practice, pleasant event scheduling will continue to move you toward healing.

You may feel that the sun no longer shines as brightly since your loved one's death. Even with the coping skills and new normal you are starting to create, your life may feel like it lacks meaning or purpose right now. At times, you may even have a desire to join your loved one in death (having plans, the means, or taking action signifies an immediate need to seek professional help). The constant yearning, loneliness, or sadness that often accompanies the traumatic grief experience can be relentless and unbearable. If you wonder if your grief has transitioned into something deeper, such as depression, see your doctor or a mental health professional.

A Deeper Dive into Self-Care

In chapter 3, we discussed the foundational role a multidimensional self-care plan has in easing the pain connected with your traumatic grief, and chapter 4 included a grief diary with space to document your self-care activities. By now, you have probably noticed some self-care actions come easily, while others are harder to achieve. You may be having difficulty making the time for, justifying the need for, or identifying self-care activities that feel beneficial in moving you toward healing. If so, it can be helpful to conceptualize your self-care plan into tiers, or levels, of action requiring different amounts of energy and producing a range of results. Similar to pleasurable events, you can think of tier-one self-care as quick and easy activities to implement in order to receive immediate, short-term boosts in your mood or energy. However, tiers two and three take more planning and investment.

Self-Care Exercise

Use the table below to organize your self-care ideas into tiers, so you have a reference list available for both short-term and longer-term self-care plans to sustain you and continually move you toward healing.

Self-Care Dimension	Tier One	Tier Two	Tier Three
Physical	Example: Take a walk	Example: Go to the doctor	Example: Train for a race
Emotional	Example: Talk with a friend	Example: Journal about your feelings	Example: Set boundaries with others
Intellectual	Example: Read a book	Example: Take a class	Example: Learn a language
Social	Example: Call someone	Example: Lunch with friends	Example: Join a book club
Spiritual	Example: Practice gratitude	Example: Meditation	Example: Attend a prayer or study group
Grief	Example: Time at cemetery or meaningful location	Example: Sit with uncomfortable feelings	Example: Join a grief group

Self-Care Dimension	Tier One	Tier Two	Tier Three
Physical			
Emotional			
Intellectual			
Social			
Spiritual			
Grief			

I encourage you to print this list from our free tool section (http://www.newharbinger.com/54926), fill it out, and keep it somewhere visible where you can reference it often. You will notice that your self-care plans and needs continuously change over time as your grief changes and evolves. You can also document your self-care activities in your grief diary by tier.

Highs and Lows

After a traumatic loss, it becomes so easy to filter every experience, interaction, and thought through the lens of grief. Therefore, at the end of day, it can be helpful to share with another person or write in your grief journal a high and low you experienced that day that had nothing to do with the pain of grief or the death of your loved one. Lows can include a flat tire, poor weather, a bad day at work, a bill, or the season finale of a favorite television show. Your highs, on the other hand, may consist of an unexpected phone call, a favorite item on sale, a drive home without traffic, or a compliment. The goal is to start expanding your ability to think about your life, even for a few more moments, outside of your grief. As you are painfully aware, the world around you continues despite the death of your loved one. Acknowledging that you too have highs and lows unrelated to grief will help you continue to move toward healing.

Gentle Reminders

Life after the sudden or unexpected death of your loved one can be exhausting, downright depressing, and awful. Watching your family and friends move on with their lives while seemingly forgetting or ignoring your pain can feel unbearably heavy at times. Observing others in your life fall in love, get married, start families, retire, and enjoy family time or life milestones —especially experiences you were meant to share with your loved one—can feel unbearably cruel. Having friends or family try and relate to your pain by sharing their own experiences, having nothing to do with your loss, can feel isolating and cause you to further disconnect. If you find yourself struggling with these experiences, I strongly encourage you to give yourself these gentle reminders:

- *Do not compare yourself to anyone else in grief.* Don't look at how you are grieving compared to others, and don't let others compare their experiences to you. Comparisons lead only to pain. Your life experiences, your loved one, their event, and your grief are highly individual. One of my favorite quotes from Brené Brown (2015, 195) states, "Stay in your own lane. Comparison kills creativity and joy."

- *You grieve the way you live.* Often clients question their behaviors in grief. "Why don't I feel comfortable doing this? Why am I not engaging in that?" The majority of the time, the behavior you are questioning or doubting was not usual or customary for you prior to your loved one's death. If you never posted about your life on social media before, you will most likely not feel comfortable posting now. If you were not one to share intimate details of your life with others, you will probably not want to start now. That does not mean you should avoid trying new or potential beneficial resources for your grief (such as support groups).

- *Grief is an expression of love.* You may have heard this before, but the depth of your grief reflects the depth of your love. The intense feelings you held for your loved one are now manifested as emotions such as pain, yearning, and sadness. In moments of deep sorrow, remind yourself that this pain is another form of love.

- *You will not always feel this way.* I know I have said this before, but it is so important it bears repeating. Despite how overwhelming, difficult, and unbearable your grief and pain are in this moment of time, it will not always hurt this much. Yes, your grief will be your companion throughout time, but it will continue to change and evolve. I have witnessed clients with intractable and overwhelming grief and pain experience significant improvements, meaning, and joy in their lives.

Use these gentle reminders when you feel overloaded or tired by your daily grief. Feel free to add additional ones of your own. In time you will not need them, as your daily burden will not feel so heavy.

Concluding Thoughts

By now you are starting to become an expert in the unwanted world of living with the daily ins and outs of traumatic grief. Each day, you are getting more skilled in living with your grief and pain. You are probably noticing that some days are easier than others, but they are still all hard.

This chapter has provided additional tools to help pace yourself for the long haul. Taking grief time-outs, scheduling pleasant events, and maintaining your self-care will be fundamental to your ability to persevere. Use distractions when needed, and more importantly, practice continued patience, love, and kindness toward yourself.

Remember your grief is constantly evolving over time, and by developing a realistic and gentle approach toward grief, you will feel more confident in your new skills and feel less overwhelmed by your struggles.

In the next chapter, we will focus on developing strategies for death anniversaries, holidays and life events, and continued periods of intense grief days.

CHAPTER 6

Prepare for Difficult Times

When you are living with traumatic grief, every day can feel like a challenge, but there are times when the pain of grief intensifies and becomes excruciating. One moment, you can be having a good day and then, seemingly out of nowhere, your traumatic grief becomes so unbearable you can no longer function. The anticipation of holidays and life celebrations may also cause significant distress. You may notice physical and emotional sensations, such as quivers in your stomach due to anxiety or dread, thinking about upcoming events. Watching others you care about move on with their lives may be agonizing to bear witness to, especially if you feel forgotten or ignored in your grief. This chapter will help prepare you for and cope with ongoing and future challenging circumstances. You will learn how to predict and cope with grief triggers, plan and prepare for difficult events, and care for yourself during these times without your loved one by your side.

After the death of your loved one, you will experience external and internal stimuli that trigger feelings of grief. Grief triggers come in all shapes and sizes and are the result of a sensory, situational, or emotional stimulus that brings grief to the forefront of your mind. You will be able to anticipate some of your triggers and may become anxious about potential bittersweet memories or intense grief, especially early on. These triggers can include birthdays, anniversaries, life events, holidays, places you visited with your loved one, photos, or a reminder of the way they died.

Unfortunately, there are triggers that will catch you completely off guard and are impossible to predict. Unexpected triggers can include hearing your loved one's favorite song while listening to the radio, watching a movie scene that sparks a memory, or walking through a store and smelling a fragrance that reminds you of your loved one. Grief triggers can elicit flashbacks, painful memories, or intense feelings of grief or trauma also known as grief attacks.

Grief Attacks

Regardless of the amount of time that has lapsed since the death of your loved one, you will experience unexpected, intense waves of emotions or what is often referred to as a *grief attack* or a *sudden temporary upsurge in grief* (STUG), a term coined by grief researcher and clinician Therese Rando, PhD. Grief attacks, like panic attacks, are often rooted in anxiety. Some people describe them as severe anxiety, panic, or overwhelming emotions that take over. Others portray their experience as debilitating waves of sadness, grief, or yearning. A grief attack is your body's way of trying to cope with the separation distress you are experiencing and may be more likely to occur when your reserves are low (for example, you are fatigued or your stress level is high). They may also represent unprocessed grief and be a part of coming to terms with your loss.

When you are early in the grieving process, your acute grief may feel like a constant grief attack, keeping you outside your window of tolerance. After a while, you will notice they become shorter in duration, less frequent in nature, and lessen in intensity. You will also be more prepared to recognize and cope with grief attacks, and when they do occur, be able to minimize the negative impact they have on your ability to function. Preemptive grief work, such as journaling, conversations with deceased loved ones, meditation, grief groups, and self-care, might also decrease their frequency.

Grief attacks can occur at inopportune times and settings. Having a predeveloped set of responses, or coping mechanisms, when you feel a grief attack begin can be instrumental in getting through these challenging times. I encourage you to review and use the care plan you developed in chapter 2 with tools to help regulate your emotions during a grief attack. You may also be able to soothe yourself with the objects, sounds, and smells you identified in your safety list in that chapter as well.

Cognitive reframing can also be a helpful tool to use when having a grief attack. *Cognitive reframing* is a technique utilized in cognitive behavioral therapy (CBT) to change unhelpful patterns of thinking into more constructive or beneficial ones (Clark 2013). When it comes to a grief attack, you can use cognitive reframing to shift your mindset and reframe the grief attack in a more positive or neutral manner. For example, at the onset of a grief attack, you can try using statements such as *I know this is temporary, I can get through this*, or *tomorrow will be a better day* to cope with your intense feelings and emotions. Clients I have worked with offered these examples of what has helped them: "I moved onto the floor and cried," "I got in bed with it," "I wrapped myself in a blanket until it was over," "I welcomed the grief attack because it knew I needed it," "I just waited until it was over," "I sat with my cat," "I held a stuffed animal," and "I pulled the car over, listened to the radio, and waited."

Use the space below to identify some of your immediate thoughts that arise during a grief attack or intense moments of distress. Next, reframe your thought into a neutral or positive statement to help you cope.

Example:

Immediate response: I cannot cope with a grief attack.

Reframed response: My grief attack is not pleasant, but I can get through this.

Immediate response: _____

Reframed response: _____

Immediate response: _____

Reframed response: _____

Immediate response: _____

Reframed response: _____

Sometimes, just letting yourself sit with the grief is all that is needed. According to Robert Niemeyer, PhD, the unanticipated anguish that overcomes you during a grief attack after a tragic loss, when least expected, can invite a self-compassionate response. Niemeyer encourages leaning into your ability to self-sooth and identifying others who are capable of supporting you during intense moments of grief, in order to gain greater equilibrium and clarity moving forward (Robert Niemeyer, email message to author May 31, 2024).

Holidays and Special Days

Holidays, anniversaries, birthdays, and life events, including graduations, weddings, or the birth of a child, can trigger a powerful grief response. Holidays and significant life milestones are often moments when being with your loved ones is most precious. These occasions are meant for embracing traditions, reminiscing about shared memories, preparing cherished recipes, and enjoying special foods together. They offer a welcome break from everyday obligations, and the absence of a loved one during these times is often deeply felt. When you're grieving, the demands of daily life can be overwhelming, and the idea of celebrating may feel not just foreign but almost cruel.

It is common to experience anxiety and dread leading up to the holidays, especially in the first few years after your loved one's death. Holidays usually encompass traditions and rituals associated with feelings of comfort and belonging. Traditions passed down from prior generations provide opportunities to recreate memories with loved ones and are chock full of rituals that provide meaning in ways we recognize, know, and cherish. These traditions and rituals are associated with stability, a sense of belonging, and community. They offer a sense of identity and a connection to your past and a bridge to future generations.

When your loved one is not present to participate in these activities, their absence can result in deep feelings of emptiness and despair. The birth of a new child, graduations, marriages, and other special occasions, meant to be joyful events shared with your loved one, can feel tainted and bittersweet. As a result, your grief can go into overdrive. The connections you have relied on can feel jeopardized, and traditions may no longer feel stable. Secondary losses are often coupled with the persistent reminder that your loved one is no longer present and that everything in your life has changed and not for the better.

If the thought of engaging in traditions without your loved one feels insurmountable, I encourage you to use special events or holidays as an opportunity to start something new. This can also be a chance to involve younger generations in creating new ways that will hold fast in the future and give you a way to honor the memory of your loved one. Your first step is to identify traditions or rituals that you want to keep and those that no longer serve you. Reflect on the cherished traditions you uphold and the meaningful rituals you share with family or friends. Which of your traditions or rituals continue to hold significant value and deserve to be continued? Doing away with those traditions that no longer serve you provides an opportunity to create something different. You might find it comforting to incorporate your loved one's favorite things, acknowledge their memory, or perform an act of service in their honor. Examples of new traditions can include:

- Making your loved one's favorite foods

- Saying prayers or toasts to their memory

- Setting a place for them at the table

- Sharing favorite stories or memories about them before a meal or dessert

- Hanging loved one's holiday stocking and writing notes for them inside

- Volunteering or supporting a cause that was important to them

- Lighting a candle in their honor

Use the following space to identify some changes you would like to make in your holiday traditions.

Holiday/Life Event	Traditions to Keep	Traditions No Longer Needed	New Traditions
Example: Christmas	Open one present Christmas Eve	Aunt Betty's surprise salad, caroling	Make Dad's dessert and tell his jokes
Example: Mothers' Day	Mothers' Day Brunch	Mom hosting brunch	Go out to brunch, Flowers from each of the kids instead of dad
Example: Graduation	Invite the entire family	N/A	Have a chair for Dad at ceremony

The creation of new traditions and rituals can be a therapeutic means of incorporating your loved one's memory into holidays and special events. Although they will still not be physically present, when you integrate their absence in meaningful ways, it can ease your grief.

Preparing for Difficult Times

If you find yourself approaching a holiday or event with intense sadness or dread, it might be constructive to examine the meaning you have attached to the day. I invite you to step back and assess the significance of the holiday or event that is worrying you and ask yourself:

- What does this day mean to me right now?

- Is there something I want to feel, celebrate, or acknowledge at this time?

- Is there purpose to this day right now in my life?

If you can identify a purpose or meaning for your holiday or event, then it becomes easier to set an intention for what you would like to experience even while grieving. Your intention may include:

- Providing your children with a good holiday experience

- Celebrating the religious significance of the day

- Acknowledging the memory of your loved one

Finally, identify the action steps you need to take to meet your intentions. This may include asking for assistance from others, making travel plans, or shopping for gifts. Action steps are also a form of self-care to make sure your grief needs are met during difficult times. Examples include:

- Going to visit friends or family

- Spending the day in church or a religious environment

- Limiting the amount of time spent around grief triggers or difficult people

Holiday/Life Event Exercise

Use the space below to identify the meaning, intentions, and action steps you can take to best care for yourself during holidays or other meaningful life events.

Holiday/Life Event	Meaning	Intention	Action Steps
Example: Easter	Time to be with family and eat good food	Enjoy grandkids, make Easter baskets	Get Easter basket supplies, make table decorations
Example: Loved one's death anniversary	Worse day ever, the day my life ended	Go to cemetery, be with close friends and family	Call best friend and ask her to make arrangements with group of close friends

Holiday celebrations and life milestones will be bittersweet experiences for a long time after your loved one's death. When you spend time thinking about these days in advance and with intention, it can make them easier to endure. Allow yourself to feel the sorrow and grieve for your loved one, but, when appropriate, also give yourself permission to be present and partake in the joy of the moment.

After a traumatic loss, your grief can feel like a life sentence without the possibility of parole. Besides having to confront holidays and the milestones in your life, it can also be painful to watch friends and family get married, have children, buy homes, go on vacation, get promoted, and continue with life when it feels like you are sitting on the sideline. Part of you wants desperately to be happy for those you care deeply about, but the other part of you hurts badly.

When your loved one abruptly died, part of your future suddenly died as well. Watching those you care about continue to engage in activities that you may have envisioned for yourself can leave you feeling robbed, cheated, and angry. Have compassion for yourself during this time. Although you care about those who are moving on with their lives, allow yourself to feel both the sadness and envy. Don't give up hope. Allow yourself to be open to future possibilities for your life as well.

Strategies for Holidays and Difficult Days

Use the following self-care tips and strategies to manage your fear or anxiety about challenging holidays or difficult days you have ahead:

- *Remember a holiday or special event is just another day.* The sun will rise, and the sun will set every twenty-four hours just like any other day. Discourage yourself from going down a negative rabbit hole or making the day bigger than it needs to be.

- *Most people find the anticipation to be the harder than the actual day.* The overwhelming majority of the clients I have worked with describe the days leading up to a holiday or life event filled with worry and anxiety; they experience a sense of relief once the day has arrived.

- *A plan for difficult days is essential.* It is important to decide prior to a holiday or event what you would like to do, who you would like to be with, and where you would like to be. You can always scrap your plan at the last minute, but waking up without a plan can be a recipe for disaster.

- *Divide your day between mourning and celebration.* This can be helpful for occasions are that are more celebratory in nature, such as birthdays and anniversaries. Sometimes, visiting a cemetery or engaging in grief work in the early part of the day will give you the emotional permission you need to experience positive feelings later in the day.

- *Communicate your feelings or fears with close family and friends.* If you are able to share your concerns or anxieties with others, they may be better able to support you and help meet your grief needs.

- *Don't be afraid to set boundaries with family or well-meaning friends.* Those who care about you may be insistent you participate in activities outside of your comfort level. Saying no is an important part of caring for yourself and your grief during holidays and difficult times.

- *Give yourself permission to skip holidays and special events.* If you find something too difficult, allow yourself to pass on participating. There are places you can go that do not embody a holiday, and people who love you will understand if you decide not to attend a special event. Just because you decide not to acknowledge a holiday or special event this year does not mean you will always decide to do it this way. Similarly, allow yourself to make decisions at the last minute or change your mind.

Concluding Thoughts

When you think about how to approach the holidays and special events, I encourage you to remember that simplicity may foster healing. Enter these difficult days with purpose and with intention, so that activities you choose feel more manageable and the emotional experiences are spread out. You now have a wide array of skills and tools to use during intense periods of grief and the means to plan for difficult times ahead.

Remember that holidays and other life events will pass and that the pain will not always be so intense. Whether you give yourself permission to ignore or permission to celebrate, death reminds us of the fragility of life. Choose to engage in meaningful activities that allow you to remember and celebrate your loved one and honor your grief needs. Be gentle with yourself and tender with your emotions. What you choose to do this year does not have to be permanent, and you can choose differently next year.

Although you may not yet be convinced, over time, holidays and special events do get easier. Trust the process and surround yourself with people who continue to accompany and support you through difficult moments.

In the next chapter, you will have the opportunity to start examining your life through new lenses and develop a long-term relationship with your grief.

CHAPTER 7

Explore Long-Term Grief

Traumatic grief is a lasting experience. To help you prepare for the long-term road ahead, it is advantageous to think about entering into a relationship with your traumatic grief. Relationships are an investment of time and energy, and by developing relationship skills you will gain the tools necessary to coexist with your traumatic grief. At times, living with the loss of your loved one will seem very doable, but in other moments, it will feel like an unbearable struggle. Fortunately, the difficult moments will continue to decrease in frequency, and by developing a relationship with your traumatic grief, you will learn techniques to cohabitate and live side-by-side together.

The death of your loved one will have a lasting impact on your identity and life path in ways you never could have imagined. Immediately after your loved one died, it was impossible to predict or comprehend the wide range of secondary losses and changes that would occur in your life. Now that your acute grief has begun to dissipate, and you are able to start reengaging with your life roles and responsibilities, the extent of these changes may have become clearer. This chapter provides you with insights and skills to equip yourself for a long-term relationship with your grief and to understand how you have changed since the death of your loved one.

Use Narrative Therapy to Develop a Long-term Relationship with Your Grief

Tenets from narrative therapy can be useful in building a long-term relationship with your grief. *Narrative therapy* is a form of psychotherapy that encourages the rewriting of life stories to live in a more balanced and compassionate manner. It operates on the principles that you are distinct from your problems and that your identity is composed of multiple, interconnected narratives. These narratives include stories about yourself and your relationships, abilities, self-worth, work, and other aspects of your life (Rice 2015). While some narratives are beneficial and promote well-being, others can lead to mental distress.

Techniques used in narrative therapy aim to deconstruct your negative or unhealthy stories and empower you to reauthor new, healthy stories with different outcomes and meanings (Hutto and Gallagher 2017).

One of the techniques used in narrative therapy is to separate, or externalize, the problem you are experiencing (Rice 2015). Externalizing your traumatic grief and viewing it as something separate from you can better position you to develop a long-term relationship with it. This process can also make it easier to examine the stories you are telling yourself about how grief has changed your life and who you are as a person. Immediately after your loved one's death, you may have felt inseparable from your grief and consumed by the intensity of your pain twenty-four hours a day. With the passage of time, you may find it easier to create distance between yourself and your grief.

Your Grief Roommate

One way to externalize your grief is to envision it as a messy, noisy, and uninvited roommate. A roommate you are unable to evict, a roommate for life. On the other hand, your grief roommate may also feel more like a loving companion, an old friend, or a guide. Its presence may be bittersweet. Some days comforting and calming, other times a sad reminder of what is no more. Your traumatic grief roommate or companion moved into your life, without an invitation, and has announced it is here to stay. The way you choose to externalize and view your roommate will most likely be influenced by the relationship you had with your loved one and the circumstances that ended their life.

Regardless of the type of roommate you now have, every long-term relationship will have its ups and downs. At times, this relationship may feel manageable and even comforting, while at other moments, it may become challenging and demanding. Almost every relationship encounters issues such as boundary violations, poor communication, unmet responsibilities, neglect, or inconsiderate behavior. Your relationship with your grief roommate is no exception. Fortunately, there are strategies to help you manage and sustain a long-term relationship with it, making grief more bearable and the relationship more constructive.

To have a successful long-term relationship with your grief roommate or companion, you will have to pay attention to both of your needs. Reflect on the ways you have learned to regulate your emotions and care for yourself during intense moments of grief. Over time, your ability to listen and respond to your body's physical and emotional needs has increased. Now that you are living with your roommate, with independent needs, you can better learn to coexist in a manner that is advantageous to you both. Your roommate will most likely act out when its needs are not being met. It is therefore mutually beneficial to learn how to best tolerate, respect, and meet each other's needs.

You know when your grief needs a time-out, rest, a distraction, TLC, and nurturing. When you work with and not against your roommate, living together will be is easier. The following set of exercises will help you better understand your grief as an independent entity, so you can develop a long-term relationship that is mutually advantageous and allows you to live together with maximum unity.

Use the space below to externalize, or remove, your grief from within by answering the prompts. These prompts are designed to help you visualize your grief. Feel free to write or draw your responses.

What does your roommate or companion look like? What is its color, shape, smell, or texture? How would you describe its personality or mannerisms?

_____

_____

_____

_____

_____

_____

_____

Spend some time observing your roommate or companion. Find out what makes it tick. How does it behave and react during everyday circumstances and intense moments?

_____

_____

_____

_____

_____

What is the hardest time of day for your roommate or companion? The easiest? How do you know?

_____

_____

_____

_____

When are they neediest? How do you know?

_____

_____

_____

_____

How do you know when they have fallen asleep or have gone out for a while?

_____

_____

_____

_____

What soothes or comforts your roommate or companion when they experience pain or distress?

_____

_____

_____

_____

What upsets them the most?

_____

_____

_____

_____

How do they behave when other people are around compared to when you are alone?

_____

_____

_____

_____

Describe any other patterns or behaviors you have noticed about your roommate or companion.

_____

_____

_____

_____

Now that you have a better understanding of your grief roommate or companion, think about different tools that you can use to better reside and even thrive while living together. It may be helpful to remember that the key to any good relationship involves compromise and a mutual understanding of your partner's needs. Examples of tools include empathizing with one another, setting boundaries, journaling for acceptance of the relationship, expressing your emotions and feelings, scheduling grief-free time, reminding yourself to be calm and patient with each other, and maintaining healthy eating, exercise, and sleep habits.

Make a list of tools you'd like to use to help create a healthy relationship with your long-term grief.

_____

_____

_____

_____

_____

_____

Living with a long-term grief roommate or companion was never something you imagined or planned. However, investing in your relationship and developing intentional ways to live together is vital to your healing process.

Traumatic Grief Changes Your Life

The consequences of your loved one's death impact every area of your life. Secondary losses are noticeable in your life domains, which include your work or school, physical and mental health, relationships with family and friends, intimate or romantic relationships, the environment where you live, financial resources, fun and recreation, spiritual/religious beliefs, and personal growth. In addition, you most likely noticed changes in how you felt at home, in your ability to participate in the activities you enjoy, or a lack of desire to explore anything related to self-improvement or personal growth.

After a loved one's death, most people struggle to connect with people, activities, and places previously important to them. As a result, you may now have started to notice deep-rooted changes that have occurred in the way you behave, think, or believe. For example, it is common to lose interest in the things that used to bring you pleasure. It is natural to feel like you are " just going through the motions every day" or that you are frozen or stuck in time. Living with traumatic grief and its unwelcomed changes can make it difficult to find meaning, purpose, or connection.

The changes that occur in response to acute grief immediately after the death of your loved one differ from the long-term consequences of traumatic grief. Now that some time has elapsed, you may be able to examine changes in your life from a different perspective. You may be ready to start exploring the purpose of pain and suffering, questioning life's meaning, or examining your faith at a deeper level. The grief and absence of your loved one remains painful and forever present, but it is possible to view these changes in your life differently.

Not all the long-term impact associated with traumatic grief is negative in nature. You may have started to implement positive lifestyle changes, make improvements at work or home, restructure relationships with family and friends, or adjust the direction of your future. You may also notice an increase in your ability to connect with others on an emotional or intimate level or a desire to engage in new work that you consider to be more fulfilling. Grief can be an opportunity to implement alternative behaviors and an opportunity to make changes or different choices when things are not serving you well.

How Grief is Changing You

As you think about the acute and continued impacts of your traumatic grief, I encourage you to take the time to reassess your traumatic grief symptoms and then to document how your loved one's death has affected each of your life domains.

Retake Grief Symptom Assessment

Before completing the exercise below, I highly recommend you retake the assessment in chapter 2, "Assessing Your Traumatic Grief Symptoms," which can be downloaded at http://www.newharbinger.com/54926. The assessment was developed to be used multiple times throughout your grief experience to help you track and monitor your grief and trauma symptoms. Once you retake the assessment, compare your responses from the initial time you completed the assessment. You will likely find these comparisons insightful.

Document Acute and Long-Term Impacts of Grief

Use the chart below to document how your loved one's death has impacted each of your life domains immediately after the death of your loved one (acute impact) and now, after the passage of time (long-term impact). In the final column, indicate whether your life domain has improved, stayed the same, or gotten worse when you compare your acute and longer-term grief experiences. Two questions after the chart will help you identity changes you want to embrace or modify.

Life Domains	Acute Impact on Grief	Long-term Impact on Grief	Identifiable Changes (improved, same, worse)
Work or school	Example: No interest and unable to work	Example: Can work, but no longer care about job	Example: Improved, realized need to find more fulling work
Physical and mental health			
Relationships with family and friends			

Life Domains	Acute Impact on Grief	Long-term Impact on Grief	Identifiable Changes (improved, same, worse)
Intimate or romantic relationships			
The environment where you live			
Financial resources			
Fun and recreation			
Spiritual/religious beliefs			
Personal growth			

Which changes in your life are serving you well and you want to continue embracing?

_____

_____

_____

Which changes in your life would you like to modify?

_____

_____

_____
_____

Even when positive changes have occurred, most people would prefer to have their loved one back by their side. Given that the return of your loved one is not an option, it is helpful to periodically reexamine the changes that are occurring in your life to determine the impact on your overall well-being. It is also valuable to identify areas where you would continue to benefit from additional intervention.

Changes in Your Identity

In addition to changes in your life domains, your loved one's death also changed your identity—who you are at the very core, your being and your soul. Your identity encompasses how you perceive yourself, describe yourself to others, and think about your physical attributes, personality, professional persona, and worldview. It is shaped by your inner self and all your past experiences, including how your family, culture, and society raised and socialized you. Your identity is continuously evolving.

Your loved one's death profoundly transformed your identity. Part of your identity was defined by the relationship you had with your loved one and roles you played within the context of that relationship, such as being a spouse or partner, child, parent, sibling, or friend. Since their sudden departure, you may feel an internal hole as you grapple with life without them, striving to forge a new sense of identity. Your challenges can include learning different roles, finding a new sense of purpose, and reflecting on your values and priorities that may no longer align with the person you used to be.

Changes in your identity are evident in the narrative, or stories, that you tell yourself and others in the absence of your loved one. These narratives include how your loved one's death has impacted who you are, your life view, and your perceptions of your future possibilities. Shifts in your identity are also shaped by those around you and reinforced by societal and cultural norms about grief. You may be able to integrate parts of yourself that existed prior to your loved one's death, or your new self may be overwhelmed by the story of how your loved one died. It is valuable to step back and examine the stories you tell yourself to ensure they correctly reflect who you are and how you want to be portrayed. After your loved one died, it can become so easy to get caught or lost in your loved one's story and feel like you have disappeared.

The following questions will help you discover the narratives you have created about your traumatic grief experience and the impact it has had on your sense of identity.

What stories have you have created about yourself since your loved one died?

_____

_____

_____

_____

_____

_____

What are the contributing factors that shape your stories?

_____

_____

_____

_____

_____

_____

How did you describe yourself to others before your loved one died?

_____

_____

_____

_____

How do you describe yourself to others now, after your loved one's death?

_____

_____

_____

_____

Who are you now without your loved one?

_____

_____

_____

_____

What parts of yourself would you like to further explore?

_____

_____

_____

_____

_____

Your identity is not static. The traumatic death of your loved one has introduced a plethora of new internal and external experiences, challenges, and interactions that are greatly influencing your evolving self. You have the option to rewrite and create a new narrative as you continue in your grief journey. The process of self-discovery allows you to reinterpret and change the stories about who you are and the impact your loved one's death has had on you. The grief work you are currently engaged in will also play an important role in contributing to future evolutions of your narrative.

Concluding Thoughts

Your traumatic grief will always be a part of you, but you now have tools to develop a long-term relationship with your grief and to respect and honor its needs, so the two of you can coexist and live in better unity. You are not your grief, and by externalizing the grief from within, you can start to live separate lives. Although grief has changed you internally, not all of the changes have been negative. Embrace the positive decisions that you have been able to make and continue to focus on the areas you identified as needing improvement.

Examining your grief narrative is a meaningful way to identify the stories you are telling yourself about the death of your loved one and who you are today. You have the power to rewrite your narrative at any time to change the factors contributing to your stories. Learning who you are and how grief changes your identity is a powerful but lengthy process you have just begun to examine.

You will continue this process of self-discovery in future chapters when you explore the concepts of meaning, purpose, and healing in grief.

CHAPTER 8

Challenging Emotions Often Present in Traumatic Grief

Some of your emotions will be intensified by the way your loved one died. During your grief, it is natural to spend time reviewing the course of events that occurred and to contemplate what could have been done differently to change the outcome. It is also common to examine your role in these events and your perception of what, if anything, could have prevented your loved one from dying.

Depending on the circumstances of your loved one's death, you may find yourself challenged by difficult emotions, including guilt, regret, or blame. Although not everyone will experience these emotions, they are highly prevalent after a sudden or unexpected loss and add an unwelcomed burden to grief. In this chapter, you will have an opportunity to explore these emotions and the impact they may have on your traumatic grief. You will also examine the roots of and purposes that guilt, regret, and blame often serve. Self-compassion and self-forgiveness exercises are tools for working through these emotions as you move toward healing.

Prior to your loved one's death, you had the gift of time, and you probably did not realize you likely took this gift for granted. When your loved one was alive, there was time to communicate and work through your problems. There was time to engage in activities you enjoyed together, time to make changes, time to get help, and time to plan and dream about the future. If there was something left unsaid, there was always tomorrow to say it. But time stopped for you, without warning, when your loved one died, and tomorrow is no longer an option. Unfortunately, you are learning, or have learned, that death brings a finality like no other. There is no longer time for a redo. There are no further opportunities to plan, say what has been left unsaid, and do the things you always meant to do. Time ran out, and most likely, without any forewarning.

Now, it may feel like you have nothing but time. Time to rethink or replay a lifetime of stories or memories that transpired prior to your loved one's death. Most likely, you spend time thinking about your role in these stories and perhaps what you could have done differently. You may be replaying moments of your life in slow motion, carefully examining each frame, dissecting the words that you said, and looking at the actions or lack of actions you took. But unfortunately, the outcome is always the same. Your loved one remains physically gone, and you, as the griever, are left with a knot of complex emotions, often including guilt, regret, and blame.

The Role of Your Belief System

Guilt, regret, and blame share a lot of commonalities when it comes to sudden and unexpected loss. As I mentioned, not everyone will experience these emotions as part of their grief journey. There is nothing wrong with you or your grief journey if the emotions described in this chapter do not resonate with you. Everyone's story is unique. Your grief is influenced by the circumstances of your loved one's death, previous life experiences, and belief system.

The roots of guilt, regret, and blame are complex. In grief, *guilt* has been characterized as an emotional response marked by a sense of disappointment for not meeting your or your loved one's internal standards and expectations in relation to your loved one and/or their passing (Li et al. 2014; Stroebe et al. 2014). Regret and self-blame are elements of guilt and have been the most frequently reported forms of guilt in the grief literature (Stroebe et al. 2014). *Regret* refers to feelings related to unfinished matters (Holland et al. 2013) or the belief that different actions could have been taken to achieve a different outcome (Torges et al. 2008). On the other hand, in the context of grief, *self-blame* focuses on the responsibility or failure that an individual played in their loved one's death or the surrounding events (Stroebe et al. 2014).

Challenging emotions often arise when there is a disconnect between your belief system and your actions. Your personal belief system includes your values or inner standards regarding your actions or behaviors, as well as your internalized family expectations. Your belief system is also influenced by the religious, cultural, and societal norms you hold. After the unforeseen death of your loved one, you have ample time to examine and reexamine your actions, lack of actions, and relationship with your loved one through your belief system. It is important to remember, that despite your belief system, there are circumstances beyond your control that can alter the course of your life and the lives of those you love.

Guilt, Regret, and Blame

While you may intellectually grasp that there were factors beyond your control, this understanding does not eliminate the persistent guilt you may feel about actions or decisions you believe could have influenced your loved one's death. This guilt can stem from words spoken or unspoken, actions taken or omitted, and even fleeting thoughts that haunt your conscience. Guilt is often rooted in your deep-seated beliefs about what you should have been capable of doing differently.

The weight of regret may linger if you were unable to provide care, ensure protection, or fulfill expected familial responsibilities. It is also not unusual to experience *survivor's guilt*, the anguish of being alive when your loved one has died. You may find yourself grappling with feelings of inadequacy for not foreseeing, controlling, or altering your loved one's outcome, or find yourself burdened by unrealistic expectations of what you should have been able to achieve. This internal struggle, with perceived short-comings and responsibilities, intensifies the emotional toll of grief and complicates your ability to move toward healing.

It is also common to experience guilt or feelings of regret upon examining your relationship and the dynamics that occurred between you and your loved one. Like guilt, regret often surfaces when you reflect on what has been left undone or opportunities you missed with your loved one: the conversations that never occurred, the issues that were never resolved, or the relationship milestones that were never achieved or celebrated. You may also regret missing opportunities, such as times you were supposed to spend together enjoying the things that you enjoyed, or moments to express feelings of gratitude, appre-ciation, or love. You may regret the actions or opportunities that you never seized, which might have changed the course of your loved one's life. Perhaps you regret being unable to get your loved one to take better care of themselves, go to the doctor, eat better, stop smoking, or exercise more.

Since you no longer have an opportunity to do or say things differently, you may be convinced that if you would have acted differently, said something else, or tried harder, your loved one would still be alive today. Whole-heartedly, you may believe you are responsible, at fault, or to blame for your loved one's death. You may be invested in blaming yourself or utilizing your emotional energy to formulate your pun-ishment. Unfortunately, these thoughts only reinforce and strengthen any guilt, regret, or blame you may be harboring.

When you reflect on the *circumstances* of your loved one's death, it is common to express your guilt in thoughts related to your actions that include "if only I would have," "should have," or "could have." Examples include:

- I should have never left them alone.

- If only I could have gotten home a little earlier that day.

- If only I had not let them drive the car.

Use the space below to list any of the "could haves," "should haves," or "would haves" you have experienced or are experiencing about the circumstances related to your loved one's death.

_____

_____

_____

_____

_____

Acknowledging these thoughts is essential for transforming your internal dialogue about the circumstances of your loved one's death. You may also experience similar thoughts regarding the *relationship* you had with your loved one. These thoughts may focus on how you could have been a better partner, spouse, parent, child, sibling, or friend. Example include:

- I should have expressed my feelings more.

- If only I would have insisted they go to therapy, maybe they would still be alive now.

- I could have been a better role model for my child.

Use the space below to list any thoughts you have about the way you could have acted differently in your relationship with your loved one.

_____

_____

_____

_____

Identifying your active thoughts allows you to:

- Notice the impact these emotions have on your well-being

- Challenge unhealthy thoughts preventing your moving toward healing

It is important to note that often feelings of guilt and regret may also be expressed as blame. It can be easy to blame yourself or others for your loved one's death. Self-blame in the grief literature typically refers to holding yourself responsible for your loved one's death (Weinberg 1994; Davis et al. 1996) or feeling blameworthy for not meeting the standards set by yourself or your loved one (Field and Bonanno 2001).

Blame can show up as anger or feelings of responsibility for the death of your loved one. It is common to be angry at medical professionals, family members, or friends and look for negligence on their part to explain some of the circumstances of your loved one's death.

It is also common to be angry at your loved one for any role they may have played in their death. Anger at your loved one is very circumstance dependent, and you may feel uncomfortable acknowledging those feelings. Anger at your loved one can look like disappointment and sadness for things such as lack of self-care, poor decisions, or being in the wrong place at the wrong time. It is okay to be angry at your loved one. Being angry does not mean you loved them any less. We get angry with the people with love. Acknowledging and working with your anger helps the feelings pass and is a healthy part of moving toward healing.

Your most difficult challenge will likely be the blame you choose to carry. Self-blame is heavy punishment. Blaming yourself for any actions you did or did not take, things you did or did not say, or warning signs you might have ignored does not bring your loved one back. I have had countless conversations with clients convinced they are responsible for their loved one's death. Often, they have spent hours, upon hours, collecting evidence from their past to prove they are liable for what has happened and therefore deserve a life of misery. It is just not that simple.

Calling Out Blame Exercise

Take some time to think about any blame you have directed toward yourself or others regarding the death of your loved one. Use the space below to identify how blame may be expressing itself. List the wrong-doing, who you believe was responsible, what you feel now, and the effect on your well-being. It is important to note that the outcome or effect on your well-being could be another emotion that could have either positive or negative consequences to your physical or mental health. If this exercise does not resonate with you, please skip.

Wrong-Doing	Who You Blame	What You Feel	Effect on Your Well-Being
Example: Did not intervene	Sibling/self	Anger	Blame, mad at self
Example: Ended their life	Parent	Sadness	Helplessness and sorrow
Example: Operated on wife	Surgeon	Anger	Inability to let go of anger and blame

This may, or may not, be the first time you have acknowledged the emotional or even the physical burden that blame can have on your well-being. If so, how does it feel to finally recognize the immense weight you've been shouldering? Sometimes your emotions will simply dissipate after they have been acknowledged. In the next section, we will explore additional in-depth consequences of holding onto the emotions of guilt, regret, and blame and reasons you may be having such a hard time releasing some of these feelings.

Adverse Consequences

Guilt, regret, or blame may manifest as constant questioning of yourself, persistent ruminations, or feelings of failure. Research investigating the adverse effects of these emotions indicates that persistent worry and ongoing rumination can lead to psychological outcomes such as anxiety or depression (Smith et al. 2012). Self-blame has been linked to elevated rates of anxiety and depression, as well as heightened trauma symptoms following the death of a loved one, whereas guilt has been associated with more intense grief symptoms (Camaco and Gordillo 2020). Self-blame has also been identified as a negative consequence for grief-related challenges after losing a loved one (Stroebe et al. 2014).

These emotions start off as coping mechanisms to protect you from painful feelings and accepting the reality of your loss. After a while these coping mechanisms are no longer effective and can take on a life of their own. When this happens, you are caught in a darker tangle of grief and heaviness that becomes a barrier and a distraction to working through your grief.

Certain circumstances that have led to your feelings of guilt, regret, or blame may stem from actual mistakes you made, while other emotions may arise from actions you wish you had taken instead. It can be profoundly beneficial to explore and process all your feelings of guilt, regret, or self-blame. When your friends and family respond with "You are not to blame" or "You shouldn't feel guilty," they are invalidating and taking away from your experience. You have every right to your feelings. What is important is to find a way to process and work through your feelings in a healthy manner. Guilt, regret, or blame will hinder you in moving toward healing; however, shifts in your thinking will assist in working through these difficult emotions.

How to Cope with Guilt, Regret, or Blame

Living in a persistent state of guilt, regret, or blame may feel like a way to stay connected to your loved one, but it is not a healthy way. You may mistakenly perceive that by focusing on these emotions, you will maintain a stronger connection to your loved one. You may feel that if you were to abandon these emotions, it would be a betrayal to your loved one. In later chapters, we will focus on heathier ways to build sustaining connection and bonds.

Reframing Exercise

One effective way to initiate shifts in your thinking is to examine your dominant thoughts and question the intentions and motivations behind the behaviors or actions that are causing these challenging emotions. Afterward, you can begin to reframe them, a CBT technique we talked about in chapter 6, to shift your thinking from a negative to a neutral or more positive way of viewing the role you played in your loved one's death.

This exercise will help you through this process.

- In the first column, identify a challenging thought associated with the death of your loved one.

- In the second column, list the emotion or emotions, such as guilt, regret, or blame, connected to this thought.

- Next, reflect on how your thoughts and emotions are serving you or what the intentions are behind your thoughts. Write down thoughts that come to mind.

- Finally, think of a way to reframe the challenging thought or a plan of action to change your thinking.

Challenging Thought	Emotion	Reflection	Reframed Thought or Action Plan
Example: My sibling would be alive if I had insisted they got care	Self–blame	Blaming myself makes me feel depressed and unable to feel present in life. If I had done more, maybe they would still be alive.	Even if I had done more, the results could have been the same.

Be patient with yourself; changes and shifts in your thinking are typically slow. You will need time to get used to these new thoughts and adapt to the reframes in your mind. If you continue to find yourself stuck in guilt, regret, or blame even after your reframing process, I encourage you to be curious with yourself. You might find it helpful to look within and ask why you are so invested in holding onto these emotions. What purpose do they continue to serve, and what would happen if you were to let them go?

Self-Compassion and Self-Forgiveness

Self-compassion and self-forgiveness are powerful antidotes against guilt, regret, and blame. Self-compassion is about being gentle and open with yourself when you do not feel deserving. Kristin Neff, PhD, a renowned expert in self-compassion, defines *self-compassion* as maintaining a balance between increased positive and decreased negative self-responses during your struggles (Braehler and Neff 2020). She describes self-compassion as the ability to recognize and acknowledge your suffering and pain; understanding that your imperfections are not failures but instead are part of the shared human experience (Neff 2011). She further breaks down self-compassion into three tenets:

- **Self-kindness:** *Self-kindness* means treating yourself as a friend during difficult times, instead of choosing self-judgment (Neff 2011). If you are struggling with difficult emotions, you can engage in self-compassion with self-kindness, being warm and supportive to yourself, so you feel safe regardless of the decisions or actions you have made.

- **Common humanity:** A sense of interconnectedness serves as a reminder that loss and pain are not isolated events but instead are universal experiences (Neff 2011). When grappling with guilt, regret, or blame, embracing common humanity can be a powerful way to feel the presence of others and connect yourself with people who are also navigating the depths of traumatic grief.

- **Mindfulness:** When you're mindful, you remain open and present to all your emotions and experiences without becoming overly attached to your struggles (Neff 2011). Although not always pleasant, learning to sit and be with your emotions, without attachment, can help you create distance from your feelings and discover how to nurture yourself in your grieving process.

You are probably aware that you judge yourself more harshly than you judge others, and the concept of self-compassion may be extremely difficult for you when it comes to your loved one's death. However, having compassion for yourself and the circumstances surrounding your loved one's death may be the key to releasing the heavy boulders you are carrying. If you find yourself struggling with the exercises above, try applying the three tenets of self-compassion.

Pause and write in the space below how you can incorporate the three components of self-compassion into your grieving process.

Self-kindness

Example: Practice positive affirmations (The circumstances were outside of my control; I did everything I could), follow self-care plan.

_____

_____

_____

Common humanity

Example: Help others in pain, participate in support group

_____

_____

_____

Mindfulness

Example: Sit with uncomfortable feelings, meditate, walk outside

_____

_____

_____

What about Self-Forgiveness?

In this chapter, you may have recognized actions or inactions that trigger guilt, missed opportunities that you regret, or decisions for which you blame yourself. The question that remains is, can you forgive yourself? Or, more importantly, do you want to forgive yourself?

Forgiveness is a very personal concept, and your beliefs about forgiveness may change after your loved one's death. You may be in a place or moment where you are not ready to forgive yourself. That is okay. I encourage you to keep the door open in case you feel differently in the future. Even if you want to hold yourself accountable for the circumstances or a wrong related to your loved one's death, you can still be kind and compassionate to yourself throughout this process. Like self-compassion, deciding to forgive yourself is a conscious action. It is a decision that involves:

- Identifying the actions that need forgiving

- Evaluating the consequences of forgiving and not forgiving yourself

- Finding meaning in the actions or reasons to forgive

- Doing something with what you have learned

Self-Forgiveness Exercise

Follow the steps below to explore your readiness to engage in self-forgiveness. You can download this exercise in our free tool section (http://www.newharbinger.com/54926) and complete this decision tree multiple times, if you'd like.

1. Select and describe an action, inaction, behavior, or decision related to your loved one's death that you would like to assess and determine if you are ready to engage in self-forgiveness.

   _____

   _____

   _____

2. Ask yourself, what were your intentions for the action, inaction, behavior, or decision?

   _____

   _____

   i. What are reasons to forgive yourself?

   _____

   _____

   _____

ii.   What are reasons not to forgive yourself?

_____

_____

_____

3.   If you decide to forgive yourself, what would forgiveness look like?

_____

_____

_____

4.   If you decide not to forgive yourself, what are the consequences you will experience?

_____

_____

_____

5.   Do you want to forgive yourself? Why or why not? *Do not answer this question until you are 95% sure of your answer—take as much time as you need.*

_____

_____

_____

6.   Once your decision is made, what type of support do you need to live with your decision?

_____

_____

_____

7. How can you learn from this experience? How does the above information move you toward healing?

_____

_____

_____

Concluding Thoughts

Deciding to forgive yourself is a form a self-compassion. It is not an easy decision, but it can be a liberating experience, and it will move you toward healing. Go at your own pace. I encourage you to return to the self-compassion and self-forgiveness exercises often. They are pillars in the grieving and healing process.

Understanding and addressing guilt, regret, or blame may be integral components of your traumatic grief process. Although difficult, you can learn from these powerful emotions. These emotions can feel overwhelming and all encompassing, but there are ways out from underneath the turmoil. Working with and through these emotions is going to take time, but it is well worth the investment. Identifying the origin of your emotions and the grip they have on your emotional well-being is a step toward changing their influence. It is possible to reframe your inner dialogue and experience shifts in your thinking. Self-compassion and self-forgiveness are powerful ways to connect with your inner resources and move toward healing.

In the next chapter, we will explore tools for living with uncertainty and the unanswered questions often prevalent in unexpected or sudden death.

CHAPTER 9

Living with Unanswered Questions and Uncertainty

Life with traumatic grief is not only devastating, but it is also often filled with uncertainty. The unforeseen death of your loved one can leave a sea of painful, unanswered questions and uncertainty in its wake. Most of the time, the unanswered questions and uncertainty you experience are related to the circumstances surrounding how your loved one died. It can be difficult to exist in this state of ambiguity and to tolerate the distress of the unknown in addition to your grief. Unanswered questions are often associated with emotional distress and anxiety as your mind seeks to fill in the gaps and make sense of the unexplainable. Uncertainty may also arise as you continue to face the unknown aspects of your loss and grapple with a lack of closure and the challenge of fully comprehending what happened to your loved one.

This chapter explores reactions that are common in a state of uncertainty and includes tools to navigate unanswered questions and live with the ambiguity often associated with a traumatic loss. At the end of the chapter, you will return to techniques used in narrative therapy to reauthor new possibilities to your unanswered questions.

The Need for Information

One of our defining traits as a species is our quest for knowledge. As humans, we have a constant need for information. We use information to assess our surroundings, ensure safety, and avoid harm. We collect data to solve problems, make decisions, and understand the world around us. Knowledge informs us about ourselves and others and allows us to develop and share social connections and be a part of a community. Information is also vital to feeling in control, establishing order, and living with predictability. The more information we have, the more confidence we have in situations, people, ourselves, and the world at large. Although we may not always like the information we receive, having information allows us the opportunity to make decisions, process feelings, and grow.

If you lack information about your loved one's death, you are probably living with unanswered questions or feelings of uncertainty. Depending on the amount of time since your loved one's death, you may find yourself searching for information with urgency, and the inability to resolve questions may seem intolerable. Alternatively, you may be distancing yourself from the details and facts surrounding your loved one's demise because the pain is unbearable at this point in your grief. There is no right or wrong way to search, filter, or process this difficult information.

Unanswered Questions

Although traumatic and devastating, you may have all the information you need about how your loved one died. The circumstances surrounding their death may be clear and understandable. This most often occurs during a health crisis, such as a sudden heart attack or stroke. Even though you understand the physical cause of death, unanswered questions or ambiguous thoughts may remain about your loved one's final moments of life. Such questions or thoughts may include:

- Was my loved one in pain when they died?

- Did they know they were dying?

- Were they scared?

Is it also possible to comprehend the physical reason for your loved one's death but find yourself questioning their decisions or role in the events prior to their death. This may be particularly true with a suicide, overdose, or accident. In these circumstances, the search for understanding your loved one's emotional state, thought processes, and final decisions prior to their death may feel essential or urgent. Your thoughts or questions may include:

- What was going through their mind?

- What were they thinking?

- Why didn't they wait for me to come home?

- Why couldn't they hold on just a little bit longer?

You may also have questions related to the circumstances of their death including:

- Where were they last?

- Who was the last person they communicated with?

- What was the last thing they were doing?

- Who were they with?

Unfortunately, there will also be circumstances when it is not possible to identify what led to your loved one's death. The cause of death may be listed as unknown or undetermined if the physical evidence is inconclusive. In some instances, there may be clarity about the circumstances, while in other cases, you may be left without any understanding. For example, I have worked with individuals who have had loved ones die from a health crisis where the final cause of death was listed as undetermined. I have also worked with clients who have experienced the death of loved ones overseas, never to be told how or where their loved one perished. The inability to identify what caused your loved one's death can trigger questions such as:

- Were there any underlying health issues that were undetected?

- Could there have been a medical error or oversight?

- Could this have been prevented?

- Should further investigations be conducted?

If you are unaware of the circumstances of your loved one's death, you may also wonder:

- Were they alone or with someone when they died?

- Who discovered them, and how were they found?

- Will there be ongoing investigations?

- Is there more information that hasn't been disclosed to me?

The above situations often occur when you are grieving an ambiguous loss. Ambiguous losses remain unclear and often lack official proof. Pauline Boss, PhD, coined the term *ambiguous loss* and made a distinction between physical and psychological ambiguous losses (Boss 2021). The sudden or unexpected death of a loved one is considered a physical ambiguous loss if you are unable to verify your loved ones whereabouts. Examples of physical ambiguous losses include the deaths of loved ones on missing airplanes, in tsunamis, during kidnappings, or through acts of terrorism, where their deaths are never confirmed. Psychological ambiguous losses, on the other hand, include dementia, traumatic brain injury, or mental health disorders, where your loved one is physically but not psychologically present (Boss 2021). Living with an ambiguous loss can amplify unanswered questions and unresolved feelings.

Calling Out the Unknowns

A helpful exercise to work with unanswered questions is to purge them from within by writing them down. These questions seem to carry more weight when trapped inside your mind, making it easier to continuously ruminate on the unknown. Your questions may look like: *Why did this happen to me or my loved one? What were they thinking? What were they doing at this place at this time on this day?* No question is too big or too small. I encourage you to just get the questions out of your head and onto paper.

Use the space below to list *every* unanswered question you have about your loved one's death:

_____

_____

_____

_____

_____

_____

_____

Now, review your list and place an X next to each question that can be answered regardless of your readiness to confront or receive the news. Keep in mind that you can choose to seek these answers at a later time when you feel prepared. Next, circle any questions you believe can be answered only by your loved one who is no longer living. We will revisit your list of circled questions later in this chapter.

Catastrophizing

When you don't have all the answers or details related to your loved one's traumatic event, it is common to spend time worrying about what their end was like if you were not by their side. You may find yourself obsessed with circumstances related to the event or trying to connect to what your loved one might have been thinking during their final moments. As a result, you may engage in what is called *catastrophic thinking*, imagining the worst-case scenarios for all your unanswered questions. When you think about the final moments of your loved one's life or the circumstances surrounding their death, it is easy to catastrophize. Please bear with me; the reality that your loved one did not survive represents the most devastating outcome imaginable. Of that, there is no question. However, you may be engaging in catastrophic thinking about the circumstances surrounding their death that doesn't represent what really happened. It can be helpful to record your thoughts so you can examine whether you are engaging in catastrophic thinking.

Use the space below to list all of the different catastrophic thoughts you have or have had about your loved one's death.

_____

_____

_____

_____

_____

_____

_____

Of course you fear your loved one was in pain, scared, and alone and everything that happened was horrific. But, just for a moment, pause and imagine there were other possibilities as well. What if they did not experience any pain? What if they were unaware of what was happening? What if they were at peace? Perhaps, they felt your presence or the company of others. Imagine if they died knowing how much they were loved. I once worked with a client whose son was killed in a car accident, and she was distraught by the lack of information she had about his final moments of life. Her thoughts assumed the absolute worst. During our work, we listed different scenarios that could have occurred during his last moments. including the awful ones she feared. Although her questions will remain unanswered, being able to acknowledge that other possibilities and peaceful scenarios she hadn't considered yet existed, besides the worst possible, brought her some comfort.

Return to your list of unanswered questions that you circled in the previous exercise. Using the space on the next page, write a list of unanswered questions and different outcomes or answers that could have occurred in addition to catastrophic ones.

Unanswered Question	Possible Answers
Example: What was going through their mind?	Example: Nothing (unconscious), fear, panic, thoughts of loved ones, spiritual or religious beliefs, acceptance, peace

The purpose of this activity is to help you expand your thinking. You do not need to choose any of the options you identified above. Instead, try and take comfort knowing that other possibilities exist outside of the worst-case scenarios.

Living with Uncertainty Is a Form of Loss of Control

The feelings associated with uncertainty and unanswered questions can result in an intensified sense of loss of control. If you remember our exploration of the theory of shattered assumptions (see chapter 1), you'll recall that the traumatic death of your loved one often evokes profound feelings of losing control and vulnerability. As humans, we do not like to feel out of control, and the death of your loved one was something you couldn't control. It is the ultimate reminder of how little control we have in this world.

Today, perhaps more than any other time, you probably realize these assumptions once kept you feeling safe and in control. Now that you have experienced the shattering of your assumptive world, you truly understand the magnitude of life's uncertainty and the lack of control you really have. Perhaps the only thing certain is uncertainty. This knowledge can also bring you a sense of freedom or relief when you stop trying to control events that were never in your control.

Unanswered Questions and Loss of Control Have Consequences

Both uncertainty and unanswered questions contribute to a complex and painful grieving process that includes doubt and confusion. When you are unable to get the information you need or live in a constant state of ambiguity, adverse consequences can occur. The unknown can be a monumental distraction that interferes with your ability to process your emotions and grief. It can further complicate your grief and result in emotions such as anger, frustration, or distress. You may experience anxiety, feel excessive worry, or find yourself trying to control others. The inability to tolerate uncertainty can contribute to worry, anxiety, and anxiety-related disorders (Carleton et al. 2007). Uncertainty can also activate your fight, flight, or freeze response (trauma response) as you search for ways to control your experience. The following sections focus on tools you can use to increase your feelings of control while living with the unknown.

Coping Tools

One of the easiest techniques to calm feelings of chaos is to identify the things in your life that you can control. You may not be able to control large-scale life events, but you are responsible for and can control your daily thoughts, actions, and behaviors. You control what time you get out of bed in the morning, what goes in your coffee, and your daily activities. You decide what to do with your free time, the people you surround yourself with, and who influences you. You are in charge of how you choose to see and view the world, your actions, and the behaviors you take to care for yourself and others.

In the space below, make a list of things in your life you can control right now.

_____

_____

_____

_____

_____

_____

As you have also learned, there are many things in life that are outside of your control. Sometimes, it can be helpful to remind yourself of what is beyond your ability or power to influence.

Use the following space to list things you can't control.

_____

_____

_____

_____

_____

_____

_____

Once you realize what you cannot control in life, you can transition your efforts into learning how to let go or tolerate what is outside of your control. You may find a new sense of freedom when you release yourself from trying to control the impossible.

Answering the Unanswered

The desire to eliminate the distress associated with ambiguity and living in the unknown has been coined *cognitive closure* (Kruglanski and Webster 1996). Techniques from narrative therapy can be useful in achieving cognitive closure. While working through the chapter exercises, you learned there are possible scenarios to address your unanswered question besides the most catastrophic ones.

Now that you have considered various possibilities and scenarios related to your unanswered questions, it may be beneficial to create a narrative that reflects your loved one's strengths and values in a way that aligns with your belief system. When you craft your narrative around your unanswered questions, there is an opportunity to retell your loved one's story in a manner that starts to create a sense of meaning (Niemeyer and Rynearson 2022). Developing narratives that bring you peace and comfort can alleviate anxiety, reduce the distress of uncertainty, and move you toward healing.

Use the space below to write a narrative for one of your unanswered questions.

Example: When my loved one died, they knew or felt _____ because _____

_____

_____

_____

_____

_____

_____

Like it or not, you are already an expert at living with uncertainty. You have been doing it for years, possibly without even knowing it. Now that your loved one has died, your tolerance for uncertainty has most likely decreased, and you are more aware of the uncertainty in your life than ever before. Here is a list of suggestions to help you cope when your feelings of uncertainty become intolerable.

- Acknowledge uncertainty, validate its presence, and allow yourself to sit in the feelings that accompany it.

- Remind yourself that you are okay. Use affirmations or grounding exercises (refer to chapter 2 for examples) to help calm yourself if you are experiencing anxiety.

- Focus on the present moment, what you can control, and what you know. Even though things are uncertain, focus on the present and the feelings you have for your loved one.

- Notice any catastrophic thoughts in your mind. Remind yourself that there are other possibilities besides the worst-case scenario.

- Remember previous periods of uncertainty you have experienced in your life and the skills you used to cope at that time.

Concluding Thoughts

Living with uncertainty and unanswered questions after your loved one's death can be profoundly challenging. Your need for answers and information related to the circumstances surrounding your loved one's death may feel intense and intolerable. There are ways you can calm the anxiety associated with the unknown. Try and refrain from catastrophic thinking and remember there are many possible answers to the unknown. Focus on the things in your life that you can control, including the activities you enjoy, the people you surround yourself with, and being in the present.

There are some questions that may always remain unanswered. Despite your hard work, you may never be able to understand the circumstances associated with your loved one's death. I encourage you to make peace with this part of your traumatic grief and remember you are okay. In future chapters, we will explore the concept of finding meaning and resiliency in an event that your heart and head may never understand.

In the next chapter you will learn that maintaining connection with your loved in death can be a healthy part of your grieving process.

CHAPTER 10

Connect with Loved Ones in New Ways

Living without the physical presence of your loved one can feel impossible. The grief and distress you endure daily, along with the void left by their physical and emotional absence, often makes life feel unbearable. At times, you may find yourself questioning your strength and determination to carry on living. Thoughts of your loved one may continue to be painful or trigger traumatic memories and symptoms. They may also provide comfort and solace, and at times, you might even feel as though your loved one is near you. There are ways to maintain a meaningful connection with your loved one, even though they are no longer physically present.

In this chapter, you will learn it is common to experience your loved one's presence after their death. You will explore the concept of continued bonds in death and techniques to develop and nurture those bonds with your loved one. Although these concepts may seem foreign to you right now, or you may not feel ready for the material included within this chapter, I encourage you to be open to relationship possibilities or connections that may lie ahead.

Beliefs regarding the fate of loved ones after death vary widely and are shaped by factors such as your worldview, upbringing, religious and cultural perspectives, and spiritual beliefs. From the moment your loved one died, you may have continued to feel their presence or received signs that confirmed their well-being or brought you peace. I have had clients share stories of dragonflies, hawks, and doves that repeatedly appear in unlikely places at just the right moment in time that provided needed reassurance and support. Others have encountered inexplicable movements of objects, unusual noises at home, unexpected life "miracles," or a series of improbable events that seem far beyond mere coincidences.

You may also find yourself frequently talking aloud to your loved one, receiving visits from them in your dreams, or engaging in imaginative or comforting conversations with them. It is common to continue dialoging with a loved one through letter writing, emails, or verbal conversations, or even to imagine how they would advise or guide you if still alive today. I have had countless clients embarrassed to admit that they have consulted a medium or psychic to communicate with their loved one. Most initially approached the experience with deep skepticism, yet nearly all left feeling comforted by the information they received, which led them to believe they had made a connection with their loved one.

Connecting with or sensing your loved one is not for everyone. Currently, you may be unable to sense your loved one, feel disturbed by signs of their presence, or be uncomfortable engaging in communication with them after their death. There is a broad spectrum of possibilities in grief concerning how you connect with your loved one in their absence. If you do not feel your loved one's presence and wish to do so, there are ways to cultivate connection or explore an alternative relationship.

Presence in Absence

In its most basic form, *presence within absence* is the ability to feel, connect, or communicate with your loved one in their physical absence as if they were still present. This experience is not only common and normative, but it can also be deeply comforting and meaningful (Burke and Rynearson 2022). Connecting with your departed loved one's presence might include sensing your loved one's enduring love, seeking their guidance and support, reminiscing to evoke a connection, or consulting a medium. It is natural to worry or question if there is something inherently wrong with engaging in continued conversations with your loved one, imagining their presence, or maintaining ongoing rituals that you used to enjoy together. There is not.

The concept of presence within absence and subsequent research has shown that partaking in certain behaviors is not only natural but can also be adaptive to a healthy grieving process, decrease feelings of loneliness, and facilitate the formation of your new identity (Burke and Rynearson 2022). These behaviors acknowledge that the impact of your loved one's life has not diminished, but instead remains vivid and alive in memories, conversations, and the essence of their being. You may be aware of your loved one's presence through sensory experiences, such as sensing their touch or hearing their voice, or through emotional and spiritual feelings that suggest they are near you. Although perhaps bittersweet or even disturbing at times, sensing your loved one's presence can serve as a healthy way to transition from the past to the present.

You may be surprised to learn research has shown there is a continued mental representation of your loved one within the central nervous system in your body that is similar to the sensation experienced with phantom limbs (Rynearson 2022). Phantom limbs have been reported by individuals who have had a limb amputated and repeatedly report feeling pain or discomfort in an appendage that has been removed. These sensations may also occur if your loved one's death has resulted in your loss of identity, prompting your brain to actively remap and reorganize sensory information (Rynearson 2022). During grief, your brain's response to severed attachments is undergoing emotional, cognitive, and social processes aimed at adapting to your loved one's loss and reorganizing emotional and physical connections.

In the space below, document any experiences where you have sensed the presence of your loved one, the feelings that arose, and reflections or thoughts you had afterward.

Type of interaction

Example: Conversation, medium, phantom limb, sign, visit

_____

_____

_____

_____

_____

_____

Feelings experienced

Example: Peace, comfort, longing, distress, sadness, fear, anxiety

_____

_____

_____

_____

_____

_____

Reflections

Example: Their presence was comforting, but my grief felt worse after their departure.

_____

_____

_____

_____

_____

_____

_____

Don't be discouraged if you have not been able to feel or sense your loved one's presence. This may happen because your beliefs about life after death are inhibiting you from feeling the presence of your loved one. For example, if you believe that your loved one ceases to exist at any level after their death, it may be difficult to feel their existence now that they are no longer living (Burke and Rynearson 2022). You may not experience their presence if you had a difficult, contentious relationship with them or there was an unresolved conflict while they were alive. In these instances, you may not be open at this time to feeling their essence, or it may contribute to a sense of feeling stuck in your grief (Kamp et al. 2021; Burke and Rynearson 2022).

In my work with clients, I have noticed that belief systems about life after death frequently change or shift after the loss of someone dearly loved. Similarly, conflicts that used to seem unresolvable often dissipate or lose importance after a loved one is no longer living. Take time to notice any changes in your thoughts and belief system and if they impact your ability to feel your loved one's presence in absence.

Dreams in Grief

Dreaming about your loved one after they have died is another common way to feel their presence. You may dream about normal mundane activities that you used to engage in together, have detailed conversations, or just sense their presence in your dreams. Dreaming about your loved one can effect a range of reactions. For example, it may be comforting, assist with emotional processing of your grief, or trigger unsettling emotions and trauma symptoms.

Your dreams can feel so real, almost as if you could reach out and touch, feel, or smell your loved one. For a moment, you may temporarily forget they have died, and when you awake, you may be stunned by the reality that they are no longer living all over again. Friends and family may also have dreams about your loved one that they share with you, another validation of your loved one's presence. One way to look at dreams is to view them as a new way of making memories of your loved one. If you have a dream, consider writing it down in your grief journal as soon as you wake, even if it is in the middle of the night, as it is the nature of dreams to quickly fade once you become fully conscious and begin your day.

I have worked with many clients who are disappointed because their loved one has not appeared in their dreams. If this is the case, your mind might be shielding itself from their presence in your dreams to prevent a trauma response. I encourage you to be patient and give the process time. If it feels comfortable, perhaps look through pictures, reflect on memories, or write your loved one a letter at the end of the day to encourage their presence in a dream.

In the space below, summarize any of the dreams that you, family, or friends have had about your loved one. Describe any of your feelings or reactions to these dreams.

_____

_____

_____

_____

_____

_____

You can document your dreams in your daily grief journal, if you'd like. Reflecting on your dreams may help you identify reoccurring patterns or themes, provide additional information, or help you continue to feel your loved one's presence. The following list provides additional examples of activities that may also increase your ability to feel your loved one's presence in absence:

- Carry something belonging to your loved throughout the day

- Maintain communication with your loved through verbal conversation or letter writing

- Listen to your loved one's favorite music

- Look at pictures or videos

- Reminisce with family or friends

- Engage in activities where you feel their presence

- Wear a piece of your loved one's favorite clothing or jewelry

In the space below, list ideas that you can use to feel your loved one's presence.

_____

_____

_____

_____

_____

When you engage in actions intended to invite the presence of your loved one, you may experience increased feelings of grief or a resurgence of your trauma symptoms. I recommend choosing one activity at a time and monitoring your feelings and symptoms in your grief diary. It might be helpful to start with an activity that is passive, such as carrying an object or wearing an article of clothing that belonged to your loved one, rather than reminiscing or looking through photos.

Continued Bonds

Closely related to presence within absence is your ability to experience a continued bond or intentional way to maintain and nurture your relationship with your loved one. This concept emphasizes an ongoing, deliberate effort to keep the connection between you and your loved one alive. Your emotional bond is a deep connection or attachment grounded in feelings of affection, care, trust, and love. Bonds involve a profound sense of understanding, mutual support, and emotional intimacy. They can be created naturally through birth, adoption, or family relationships or formed over time through shared experiences, meaningful interactions, and sustained communication. Bonds develop in a multitude of relationships not only

within families, but also between friends, romantic partners, colleagues, mentors, and spiritual compan-
ions, as well as between humans and animals. The following examples are different types of relationships
with emotional bonds and their resulting characteristics:

- Parent-child: nurturing, protecting, and mutual dependence

- Romantic partner: intimate, passionate, companionship, understanding, and commitment

- Sibling: rivalry, camaraderie, protection, and lifelong shared memories

- Friendship: trust, loyalty, shared experiences, and support throughout the highs and lows in life

Once a bond has developed and solidified, it is difficult to destroy, even upon death. The concept of
continued bonds in grief disputes early grief theories when healing was believed to occur only after
detachment from a deceased loved one was complete. The book *Continuing Bonds* introduced the idea
that the optimal outcome in grief involves sustaining an enduring connection or bond with your loved
one (Klass et al. 1996). These bonds are profoundly shaped by the social and cultural narratives in your
life, which in turn influence your process of meaning-making in grief (Klass and Steffan 2018).

A *continued bond in death* is as an ongoing inner relationship between a bereaved individual and a
deceased person (Stroebe and Schut 1999). When you maintain a continued bond with your loved one,
your relationship changes and adjusts as part of a healthy grieving process. It is also possible to make
changes in your relationship that you were unable to achieve while your loved one was living (Klass and
Steffen 2018). Research has shown these bonds can enhance your transition to your new life without your
loved one by integrating their presence, bringing you comfort and practical support, and facilitating adaptation to the bereavement process (Hewson et al. 2023; Klass and Steffen 2018). I have seen parents
continue to engage in activities they shared with their children, such as working on old cars, playing
sports, or hiking to maintain continued bonds. I have also seen family members volunteer at homeless
shelters, donate musical instruments annually, and adopt certain eating patterns to develop or continue
bonds with loved ones no longer living.

Unfortunately, not everyone had a healthy relationship or was in good standing with their loved one
at the time of death. A difficult predeath relationship may impact your ability to develop continued bonds
or may result in bonds that are distressing (Hewson et al. 2023). It is also important to note that an over-
reliance on a continued bond with your loved one can become problematic. This occurs if the bond
prevents you from engaging in other living relationships or keeps you emersed in your grief. However,
maintaining these bonds one can facilitate a healthy grieving process by avoiding overdependence or
destructive behaviors keeping you grounded in the past.

Depending on your circumstances and the amount of time that has lapsed since the death of your
loved one, maintaining a connection or a continued bond may not be right for you at this moment. You
might be too emotionally raw or overwhelmed, a continued bond may conflict with your current beliefs,

or the circumstances may simply feel inappropriate. This is a concept you can always return to, if or when the timing feels right.

Developing Continued Bonds

There are many ways to create bonds with your loved one. Bonds can be developed or strengthened through conversations, rituals, or routines that incorporate aspects of your loved one's essence into your daily life. I encourage you to be intentional when contemplating the bonds you would like to create.

Answering the following questions may help identify new ways to strengthen or build continued bonds.

Which shared activities that you enjoyed with your loved one can you continue to pursue on your own?

_____

_____

_____

What rituals can you create to honor and strengthen the bond you shared with your loved one?

_____

_____

_____

What projects or causes were important to your loved one that you can continue to support and champion?

_____

_____

_____

How can you integrate the essence of your loved one into your daily routine?

_____

_____

_____

_____

Here are some additional examples of things you can do to maintain your relationship or bond with your loved one:

- Care for their grave site

- Nurture a garden or tree you plant in their honor and watch it grow

- Volunteer or contribute to their favorite charity or cause

- Reminisce with family and friends, pass down stories to younger generations

- Make their favorite meals or foods each week

- Engage in a legacy project (for example, write their life story or create something in their honor)

- Take on characteristics of your loved one

- Engage in activities they enjoyed or you experienced together on a regular basis

- Use your loved one as a role mode to guide your behavior

- Participate in events that honor your loved one

When the grief and trauma symptoms begin to dissipate, it can be easy to get busy and return to the everyday demands of life. Many clients have expressed their appreciation to participate in continued bond activities, as it enables them to stay connected to their loved one and honor their grief. It is also worth noting that although this chapter and the primary focus of this book has been on the relationship between you and your loved one, their death most likely disrupted your core family. You can use the concept of continued bonds and the activities listed above as ways to strengthen family ties in grief and remain connected as a family unit to your loved one who is no longer present. I encourage you to do what feels most comfortable to you at this time.

Concluding Thoughts

Maintaining a connection with your loved one after death is a natural experience and is not pathological in nature. It is common to experience your loved one's presence and to develop a long-term relationship or bond with them after they are no longer physically present. There are many ways you can communicate with, connect with, sense, or feel your loved one. I encourage you to remain open and receptive to the different possibilities if they align with your belief system and the timing feels appropriate for your grief. If you are not ready to participate in these activities now, you may return to these suggestions at a future date.

In the next chapter, you will delve deeper into the concept of healing and explore different ways to grow after the death of your loved one.

CHAPTER 11

Healing and Growing Through Your Grief

The concept of healing can seem foreign and unimaginable after your loved one's death. Your heart is shattered, and deep down you know that time cannot mend this wound. There exists a profound void in your life where your loved one once stood, and you recognize that nothing can ever fill or replace the space they left behind. As the end of this workbook draws near, the thought of healing may still not feel close enough to grasp. You may not even feel ready to read this chapter. It is okay. I encourage you to keep going, as the information in this chapter meets you where you are today.

Early on, the concept of healing was introduced as an ongoing process rather than a definitive state. Now, you will have an opportunity to define the concept of healing for yourself and explore some of the elements that you feel are embedded in your healing framework. You will discover the growing around grief model, which validates the enduring presence of your grief and the importance of new growth in your life. The five domains of post-traumatic growth will be introduced to highlight possible transformations after a traumatic event. Finally, we will explore strategies for overcoming moments when you feel stuck or immobilized in your ability to move toward healing and the importance of a healing mindset in grief.

Healing after a Sudden or Unexpected Death

By now, you have heard me repeat multiple times that the feelings you have about your loved one, the pain of their absence, and your love for them will always remain, it just won't always hurt this badly. The concept of healing in grief is personal and holds a different meaning for each individual grieving a loss. Some people define healing in grief as the absence of pain, yearning, or other grief symptoms. Others prefer to remain connected to loved ones in their grief and may describe healing as the ability to function without the help of their loved one. The journey toward healing encompasses a wide range of desired outcomes, including seeking strength, alleviating loneliness, reducing pain, or enhancing resilience. It may also include functioning more effectively, rediscovering joy, maintaining a connection with your loved one, or cultivating inner peace. There is not a right or wrong way to define what moving toward healing means for you. And, like everything in grief, the concept and journey toward healing is fluid. One day you might feel closer to healing, and other days it may feel so out of reach.

Being completely healed after your loved one has died is an impossible task. However, feeling good again, living a fulfilling life, remaining forever connected to your loved one, and experiencing joy, laughter, and love is not.

In the space below, describe your concept, definition, or thoughts about healing *at this time* in your grieving process.

_____

_____

_____

_____

Your concept of healing will most likely continue to evolve with your grief. Reflect on how you feel in this moment compared to the immediate aftermath of your loved one's death.

Describe at least three ways you have begun to move toward healing.

Examples: I can sleep through the night, I no longer experience daily flashbacks/nightmares, or I can go shopping by myself with confidence.

1. _____

2. _____

3. _____

At this point, it is so important to acknowledge any accomplishments in your healing or any new abilities you have acquired. There are countless new roles, responsibilities, and emotional hurdles that you have most likely been called to face. And, as your ability to conquer these challenges is realized, no matter how painful the process may be, your efforts need to be acknowledged and celebrated.

While "celebrated" might not be the word that immediately comes to mind, it is appropriate considering that your accomplishments most likely required immense effort. Recognizing and celebrating your efforts can help foster a sense of empowerment to help you succeed in other difficult tasks. I have witnessed clients feeling empowered by balancing checkbooks, setting traps and catching rats, enduring holidays alone, tolerating medical procedures unaccompanied, withstanding Mothers' Day after losing a child, and buying birthday gifts without their spouse. These experiences are grueling, but the fact that you can navigate them, despite your loved one's absence, is significant and should be celebrated.

The list of above accomplishments may seem menial and merely just your way of getting by. But progress and movement toward healing must start somewhere. If you are further along in your grief journey, you may be ready to explore the concept of healing on a deeper level.

A Deeper Dive into Healing

It is common to wonder *How will I know when I am better?* or *Is this as good as it gets?* These questions are not easy to answer and are complex in nature. Your healing framework may include coping and adapting, developing resilience, or growing from your traumatic grief.

Coping and adapting to the loss of your loved one involves finding healing strategies to live with the daily challenges and emotions, as you create your new normal and move forward in your life. Research shows that grief evolves over time, and you can move beyond just coping with your loss (Doka and Tucci 2018). Although you may currently feel like you are going through the motions in your life, it is possible to move beyond this phase to reengage more fully with your life and experience joy, meaning, peace, and the concept of healing you described above.

You are also resilient. Most people are psychologically resilient, even when faced with grief and trauma, and in time, you will be able to persevere and adjust to the adversity and traumatic events that accompany your loved one's death (Bonanno 2004). But even beyond resiliency, it is also possible to grow from trauma and suffering.

Growth can be any positive transformation that emerges from your loved one's death, such as gaining spiritual insights, developing a deeper appreciation for life and relationships, acquiring new knowledge, or achieving a heightened existential awareness (Doka and Tucci 2018). Your grief may transition from coping and adaptation to resilience and then growth, or you may find your healing continues in one area.

Growing Around Grief

The death of your loved one has left an immense, gaping void or an unfathomable hole in your heart. As you know, nothing can fill this hole. Although this void will always remain, its existence does not mean other areas of your life can't grow and flourish.

Lois Tonkin developed a model called *growing around grief*. According to Tonkin, your grief does not dissipate or change in size; instead, your life begins to grow around your grief (Tonkin 1996). This model emphasizes that although your grief remains the same size, over time, your world grows and expands, as seen in figure 4. Immediately after your loved one's death, your life was your traumatic grief, as illustrated by the black circle on the far left. During that time, the majority of your energy was spent navigating your grief and trauma symptoms—and just trying to get through your day. As you advance toward healing, your grief remains a stable presence, yet your traumatic grief symptoms diminish, allowing you to reconstruct your life and grow around your grief. This is illustrated in the circles on the right.

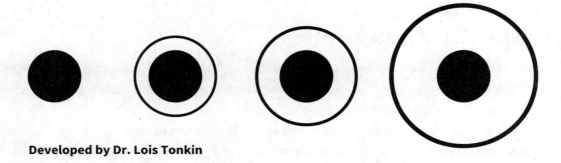

Developed by Dr. Lois Tonkin

According to the growing around grief model, your grief does not dissipate or change in size; instead, your life begins to grow around your grief (Tonkin 1996).

In the space below, list some of the ways you have started to grow around your grief. What things in your life now occupy the "white" space.

_____

_____

_____

_____

_____

The growing around grief model challenges the conventional belief that time alone heals all wounds. Time will not heal your grief. Time will decrease the frequency and intensity of the symptoms you experience, but it will never fill the gap left by your loved one's absence. Instead, as you continue to move forward in your life, bit by bit, your distractions will transition into genuine interests. It is important to note, at times, the expected and unexpected triggers you experience (as explained in chapter 6) can transport you back into the nucleus of your grief. When this happens, it can feel like you are swallowed and consumed again by your grief. However, you now have new tools and resources to cope with these challenging times. So, it may be possible to put some space between you and your loss as you function at a higher level and feel a little more like yourself.

Posttraumatic Growth

It is possible to grow from trauma and emerge transformed into a stronger, more positive state than before your trauma occurred. The aftermath of your loved one's death, including the shattering of your assumptive world, can result in profound growth. Richard Tedeschi, PhD, and Lawrence Calhoun, PhD, coined the term *posttraumatic growth* (PTG) to refer to a positive change that individuals can experience beyond just recovering or returning to baseline functioning after a crisis or a traumatic event (1995). Although the concept of growth through suffering is not new, your ability to experience posttraumatic growth will be influenced by factors such as your previous life experiences, social support, the traumatic event, and other characteristics specific to your life. I have witnessed countless clients not only move toward healing but also find themselves experiencing and exceeding expectations for enhanced growth.

Posttraumatic growth is both a process and an outcome (Doka and Tucci 2018). It is rooted in the belief that something good can come from something horrific and tragic. Tedeschi and Calhoun (2004) identified that posttraumatic growth manifests across five distinct domains:

- A heightened appreciation for life

- The development of deeper and more meaningful relationships

- Increased personal strength

- Enhanced life possibilities

- An enriched spiritual or stronger belief system

Posttraumatic growth is an individualized process, and it is not a guaranteed experience. The death of your loved one is most likely one of the worst experiences you have had and will ever encounter. But I encourage you to be open to growth and positive changes in your life. I have clients who have experienced PTG launch foundations in memory of their loved ones, transform their daily routines, cultivate greater empathy, leave jobs that caused them deep unhappiness, end toxic relationships, and move to their dream destinations. It is possible to let the traumatic death of your loved one guide you to deepen your connection to your core values, strengthen your presence in the moment, reject unfulfilling commitments, and free yourself from what no longer serves your well-being.

Circle any changes or growth you have noticed in the posttraumatic growth domains listed below. Remember, PTG usually occurs in one or two domains after the passage of time, and not everyone experiences this phenomenon.

heightened appreciation for life   *deeper relationships*   *increased personal strength*

enhanced possibilities in life   *enriched spiritual/stronger belief system*

Use the space below to describe any positive changes, growth, or thoughts you may have about PTG in general.

_____

_____

_____

_____

_____

_____

It is okay if these examples do not register with you at this point in your grief. I invite you to tuck this information in the back of your mind, and if the time is right, the seeds will sprout.

Feeling Stuck in Grief

Chances are you will have days or longer periods of time when you feel like you are regressing or going backward in your grief. It may even seem like you have returned to the very beginning of your grief experience or are not moving in a forward direction. If this happens, please remind yourself you are moving toward healing even on your hardest grief days, on the days when you do not want to get out of bed and it feels like you are sliding backward. Your grief is neither linear nor always forward facing, but it is moving. There are times, however, when you may become temporarily frozen or stuck. Don't be alarmed.

As with any difficult journey, you will plateau. Unlike other journeys, your grief is lifelong. Use this phase as an opportunity to reflect, without judgement, and be curious about the obstacles or circumstances you are encountering. Take your time. There is no hurry.

Answer the following questions if you feel stuck or frozen in your grief. You can also download this form at http://www.newharbinger.com/54926 and answer these questions whenever you are feeling stagnant in your grieving process.

What has led me to feel stuck or frozen in my grief at this time?

_____

_____

_____

What are the emotions or feelings I am currently experiencing?

_____

_____

_____

What strengths can I build on from my past experiences to help get me through this?

_____

_____

_____

What can I learn from this current experience?

_____

_____

_____

What options or resources can I use to create momentum?

_____

_____

_____

In addition to the questions above, refer to the following suggestions, if you feel stuck in your grief.

- *Monitor your thoughts to determine if you are focusing on how or why your loved one died.* It is easy to experience a downward spiral if you continually focus on the traumatic circumstances of your loved one's death. Remind yourself that the way your loved one died was only a fraction of their life. It does not represent who they were or the love you have for them.

- *Expand your support system.* There may come a time when you feel family or friends are unable to meet your needs because they don't understand your traumatic grief, are no longer as supportive, or are encouraging you to move on. Widen your inner circle. Seek out others who have experienced similar losses and can validate, witness, and support you in your continued pain and growth.

- *Redefine your concept of healing.* When feeling stuck, break down your concept of moving toward healing into smaller phases or steps. You can rewrite your definition as often as needed. Identify small, doable behavioral changes you can focus on, so you can begin to see some progress. These can include making changes in self-care, increasing socialization, or scheduling pleasant events. One of my favorite phrases is: the only way to eat an elephant is one bite at a time.

- *Identify and celebrate positive steps in your healing.* It is important to rejoice in small accomplishments and progress along the way, especially if you feel frozen in grief. Maintaining a grief diary can help identify the steps you are taking toward healing, even though you feel stuck. It is important to remember that sometimes progress can be hard to see.

- *Be of service to others.* Movement and change can also occur when you step outside of your grief and extend support to others who are also hurting. Posttraumatic growth is more likely to occur when you engage in meaningful work or have a mission to enrich the lives of others (Moore 2018).

Feeling stuck or frozen in your grief is usually temporary and a natural part of moving toward healing. If you find yourself unable to move forward after an extended period of time, or have concerns about your mental health, seek the support of a mental health professional. Often, the key to advancing through grief lies in shifting your mindset.

A Healing Mindset

I have heard numerous times "My life feels muted now that my loved one is no longer living" or "Everything looks grey." If those statements resonate with you, you are right. But those thoughts and feelings are your grief speaking. Creating a healing mindset is essential to move toward healing.

A *healing mindset* is a proactive, realistic, and positive approach to living with your grief for the long haul. It involves embracing change with openness and recognizing that growth includes both progress and setbacks. This mindset incorporates self-compassion (see chapter 8) and is a transformative approach integrating growth, resilience, and inner peace. When you have a healing mindset, you are able to sit and tolerate your feelings and discomfort without being overwhelmed. Though challenging, this form of mindset helps you view your loved one's death within the broader context of your life to avoid feeling like a victim and empowers you to continue moving toward healing and hope. A gratitude practice can be a beneficial part of a healing mindset.

Reflecting on the meaningful experiences you shared with your loved one, list five things that you feel grateful for.

1. _____

2. _____

3. _____

4. _____

5. _____

Although this list may seem bittersweet at present, being able to have gratitude for the time and experiences you shared with your loved one when they were alive is part of a healing mindset.

You are not your traumatic grief. In chapter 7, you learned how to develop a long-term relationship with your grief, and an initial step was to externalize your grief from within so you could live together, side by side. Separating yourself from your grief may make it easier to adapt a healing mindset, while discouraging your grief from speaking for you. As one of my previous clients said, "I have skin in the game and am still here for some reason." Once she was able to see herself as independent from her grief, her motivation to coexist with her grief and adapt a healing mindset increased. At times, this process will seem easier than others, and you may have to consciously choose or remind yourself that you want to continue moving toward healing.

Concluding Thoughts

Much like a deep scar, the pain and grief from your loved one's traumatic death will never fully vanish, but your healing is a continuous and evolving process. As time progresses, your life will gradually expand around your grief, allowing you to rediscover joy and positive emotions as you reinvest in living fully. Although these feelings may evolve and shift from what they once were, you will increasingly embrace and cherish them in a deeper, more meaningful way. It is possible to transform and grow from your traumatic loss, discover new opportunities, deepen relationships with others, evolve and lean on your belief system, and find new strength within yourself. Be open to these possibilities. If you find yourself temporarily stuck or frozen in grief, sit with these uncomfortable feelings, focus on your mindset, and be intentional in your actions about moving forward in your healing.

In our final chapter, you will explore how to create a meaningful future.

CHAPTER 12

Your Meaningful Future

When you're preoccupied with navigating life without your loved one, envisioning a meaningful future in their absence can seem improbable or impossible. As unlikely as it may currently seem, creating a fulfilling future is within your grasp, just not the way you originally imagined.

In this final chapter, you will explore what constitutes a meaningful future. You'll redefine concepts of happiness, fulfillment, and joy based on who you are now and how you have changed in your grief so far. You'll identify diverse ways of bringing meaning into the new life you are slowly creating, while expanding upon the ideas and insights you have gained from this workbook. To help lay the foundation for your future, you'll reflect on the activities and relationships currently in your life that add value and direction. Additionally, you'll have the opportunity to connect with your future self, guiding you in navigating and planning your path forward. The workbook concludes with a closing activity to highlight the major takeaways you have learned and areas where you would like to continue growing.

As we explored, it is impossible to predict or control your future. The death of your loved one derailed and overwhelmed you, and while you now have managed to stabilize your day-to-day life, the challenge remains: how to look forward and plan for your future. At this current time, you may not feel safe thinking beyond your everyday survival. It may be too sad or depressing. It may also feel overwhelming or exhausting. That is okay. If you are not ready to think about your future, I encourage you to skim through this chapter, so you're aware of the materials available to you when you're ready to explore further.

Letting Go of Previous Plans

Most likely, your loved one's death significantly impacted the plans you had for your future. You may have planned your retirement, had dreams of raising children or enjoying grandchildren, planned travel, and had weddings to celebrate. You may have had shared goals, conflicts to resolve, conversations to look forward to, and lives to live together. In an instant, the future you had outlined disappeared, leaving you with a sense that looking ahead now feels like staring into an abyss.

To create a meaningful future for yourself, you will need to pivot with a capitol *P*. In time, you will grieve and release the previous expectations and dreams you had in their original form, so that you can begin to make room for new opportunities and possibilities. This is a difficult request because it involves confronting something you would rather avoid. It does not mean you are letting go of your loved one. You are releasing your expectations about how things were supposed to be, because your previous plans are no longer a viable option. Instead, you are going to create a new plan that includes ways to integrate your loved one into your life while you explore new and meaningful paths forward.

List some of the plans, dreams, and/or goals that you need to release and grieve in their original form. Examples may include retirement with my partner, watching our child graduate from college, or having a child together.

_____

_____

_____

_____

_____

_____

The plans you just identified are some of the secondary losses that we explored in chapter 4. These losses can be just as painful as the actual death of your loved one because they include missed opportunities, lifelong dreams or aspirations, or the culmination of your work and love. Realize your feelings about your loved one's death may still be incredibly raw, as they impact your future visions, identity, goals, and dreams.

Grieving shattered losses will take time and intention, but it is a necessary part of moving toward healing. You might find it helpful to reframe your thoughts or think about these losses in a neutral or different way. You may also need to adjust some of the plans you had for the future or engage in a symbolic activity or ritual to help process the losses related to the future you can no longer create. For example, you could have a symbolic burial for unfilled dreams, such as watching your child graduate from college. You could also revise your dream to have a child with your partner by becoming a single parent. Additionally, you could modify certain decisions, such as postponing a retirement or choosing to volunteer to remain active, until you feel emotionally equipped to no longer be part of the workforce.

Review your list of future plans, dreams, or goals from the previous exercise and then list below ideas for grieving some of your losses.

_____

_____

_____

_____

_____

_____

I am asking you to hold hope and trust that over time there will be other ways to pursue some of the plans, goals, and dreams you had envisioned. And, if you choose, there will also be ways to incorporate your loved one's presence in your future. Creating a meaningful future for yourself includes the belief that you deserve happiness, joy, and other positive emotions, even if the experiences will be different.

Redefining Expectations and Emotions

You are not the same person you were prior to your loved one's death. Your identity, the way you interact with others, and your beliefs about the world have changed. By now, you have probably noticed the way you feel and express your emotions has also changed. Yes, you will continue to feel happiness, joy, love, and other positive emotions, but they will feel different.

Many of the clients I have worked with share that they experience happiness and joy from the smaller, simpler things in life. These include watching a child messily eat ice cream dripping down their chin, deep conversations with friends sharing intimate stories, or walks in nature marveling at the beauty of the flowers never before noticed. You may no longer find joy in activities you once enjoyed, particularly in large gatherings or social events. Instead, spending time alone now may be a positive experience for you. You may also find yourself drawn to activities that evoke emotions like peace, comfort, or relaxation.

Emotion Exercise

Select three emotions, either from the list below or of your choice, and describe what each one means to you at this moment. Identify examples of activities that you can incorporate into your life that would elicit each of the emotions you have defined.

Emotions: joy, hope, love, fulfillment, excitement, happiness, or peace

Emotion and Description	Example Activities
Example: Excitement: something I look forward to	Example: Dinner with friends, shopping at my favorite store during a sale, opening day for a good movie
1.	
2.	
3.	

Along with defining these emotions, you may need to grant yourself permission to fully experience them. It is common to deny yourself the opportunity to experience positive emotions when your loved one cannot share in or participate in those feelings (Hershfield 2023).

If you struggle to engage in activities that generate positive emotions, try taking a closer look at what other obstacles might be hindering you or holding you back. Ask yourself how you can create space for these positive emotions in your life. Building a meaningful future will involve embracing a full range of emotional experiences, and you now have additional tools to cope with the highs and lows you will continue to face in your grief.

Meaning After Traumatic Death

It is natural to seek a sense of meaning in your future by incorporating or acknowledging the impact of your loved one's death. Trying to find meaning in the traumatic event that ended your loved one's life can be challenging. The manner of your loved one's death may seem devoid of meaning; however, the significance will emerge from how you shape and build your life in the aftermath. In time, the way you choose to live your life, the relationships you sustain, the decisions you make, and the narratives you create will transform into a meaningful future.

In chapter 11, you discovered that a traumatic event could lead to profound growth. There will come a time in your healing process when you acquire the ability to intentionally transform your loved one's death into an opportunity for your growth. You may choose to share this growth or contribute to the well-being of others. Creating a meaningful future involves redefining your life and purpose in the wake of loss. This requires grieving and adapting to unwanted changes, letting go of expectations, and discovering new sources of fulfillment and hope. If you choose, your meaningful future can also integrate your loved one's memory and essence, even as you create space for new dreams, goals, and experiences.

What is Possible for You Now?

Depending on your circumstances, the death of your loved one may have created a new set of possibilities you never would have expected. A blank canvas you perhaps never wanted, but you now possess. A backdrop with space for new opportunities, experiences, and possibilities.

It can be scary to think about new options. It can be daunting to dare to dream again without a guarantee that it won't all disappear in a flash. I remember one client who said, "Why should I try again if everyone I love or could love might disappear in an instant?" Yes, hoping, loving, and dreaming again has inherent risks, but walling away your heart has equally substantial consequences. To forge a meaningful future, you must commit to fully reengaging with life. Embrace your current journey with grief as your constant companion and go all in together. Doing so does not mean that your grief attacks, yearning, or loneliness will dissipate and resolve. But it does signify you are committed to yourself and your future regardless of the intensity of your grief. You are pledging to live your best possible life despite your sudden or unexpected loss.

Developing Your Plan

It is natural to have difficulty envisioning your future without your loved one's presence. Trying to imagine your life, years from now, often leads to an empty mind. Instead, you may find it easier to focus on different areas of your life that are important to you, activities that you enjoy, and relationships that bring meaning to your life. Being aware of your level of satisfaction in your different life domains can help you identify areas where you'd like to start.

Assess Your Life-Domain Satisfaction

Think about each of your life domains (listed in the first column) and circle the number that represents how satisfied you are. For example, if you just experienced the death of your spouse or partner, you would most likely circle a 1 in the domain of "intimate or romantic relationships" to indicate you are not at all satisfied.

Life Domain	Level of Satisfaction
Work or school	1 .... 2 .... 3 .... 4 .... 5 .... 6 .... 7 .... 8 .... 9 .... 10 *Not at all satisfied* *Extremely satisfied*
Physical and mental health	1 .... 2 .... 3 .... 4 .... 5 .... 6 .... 7 .... 8 .... 9 .... 10 *Not at all satisfied* *Extremely satisfied*
Relationships with family and friends	1 .... 2 .... 3 .... 4 .... 5 .... 6 .... 7 .... 8 .... 9 .... 10 *Not at all satisfied* *Extremely satisfied*
Intimate or romantic relationships	1 .... 2 .... 3 .... 4 .... 5 .... 6 .... 7 .... 8 .... 9 .... 10 *Not at all satisfied* *Extremely satisfied*
The environment where you live	1 .... 2 .... 3 .... 4 .... 5 .... 6 .... 7 .... 8 .... 9 .... 10 *Not at all satisfied* *Extremely satisfied*
Financial resources	1 .... 2 .... 3 .... 4 .... 5 .... 6 .... 7 .... 8 .... 9 .... 10 *Not at all satisfied* *Extremely satisfied*
Fun and recreation	1 .... 2 .... 3 .... 4 .... 5 .... 6 .... 7 .... 8 .... 9 .... 10 *Not at all satisfied* *Extremely satisfied*
Spiritual/religious beliefs	1 .... 2 .... 3 .... 4 .... 5 .... 6 .... 7 .... 8 .... 9 .... 10 *Not at all satisfied* *Extremely satisfied*
Personal growth	1 .... 2 .... 3 .... 4 .... 5 .... 6 .... 7 .... 8 .... 9 .... 10 *Not at all satisfied* *Extremely satisfied*

Take a minute and reflect on your answers and the numbers you have circled. Identify the three life domains where you feel the least satisfied (lowest numbers). Outline specific actions below that you can take to enhance your satisfaction with each of the three domains you selected. You can also change the exercise to outline actions you want to take to improve your satisfaction with the life domains where you're most satisfied (highest three numbers). If one of your lowest domains was directly related to the death of your loved one (romantic relationships due to the death of your partner or spouse, or family relationships due to the death of family member), you may want to choose another life domain.

Outline specific actions below that you can start taking to enhance your satisfaction with each of the three domains your selected.

_____

_____

_____

_____

_____

_____

_____

Part of this process is learning and exploring yourself in new and different ways in the absence of your loved one. It is possible your future might embrace new interests, develop a diverse new skill set, or explore unfamiliar activities.

Answer the following questions, which may stimulate alternative thoughts to create a meaningful future that incorporates your interests, values, and your loved one.

What brings you joy or happiness right now?

_____

_____

_____

What gives you a sense of purpose or fulfillment?

_____

_____

_____

Which of your past goals or dreams can still be achieved with a new perspective or other adjustments?

_____

_____

_____

Is there something you've always wanted to do, but life previously got in the way? Do your current circumstances now make it possible?

_____

_____

_____

What types of relationships do you aspire to have with other people, and what role would you like to see your grief play in those relationships?

_____

_____

_____

_____

How much do you want your grief to be part of your future life, and how do you want to experience or express it?

_____

_____

_____

_____

How do you want to integrate your loved one's memory, presence, or essence into your future?

_____

_____

_____

_____

Your Future Self

One way to connect with your future is to have an imaginary conversation with a future version of yourself or to write your future self a letter. You can experience a positive impact on your present well-being when you connect with a future version of yourself (Hershfield 2023). Now granted, this exercise will not resonate with everybody, but I encourage you to give it a try. You have nothing to lose.

To have an imaginary conversation with a future version of yourself, get in a comfortable position, shut your eyes, and relax your body with a series of deep breaths. Choose a time period in the future that ranges anywhere from one to ten years from now. Imagine the geographic location where your future self lives: the neighborhood, home, and outdoor space. Visualize yourself in your current state, knocking on the door, and your future self welcoming you in. What are they wearing, and how do they appear? What do they look like? Happy? Sad? Grief-stricken? Are they content or at peace? Imagine yourself engaging in a conversation with your future self. Ask them how they are doing. Be curious about what their life experiences have entailed. What is their grief like now? How have they grown? When you are ready to leave, ask them what you need to know to get from where you are now to where they are in the future.

Describe details of your conversation.

_____

_____

_____

_____

_____

_____

If visualizing your future self wasn't effective, try writing yourself a letter to be opened at a future date. In this letter, articulate the aspirations and goals you hope to achieve and express your thoughts on where you envision yourself when you read it. Reflect on the hopes, dreams, and future ambitions you want to manifest. Additionally, consider including expressions of gratitude for the people, experiences, and things you cherish, as well as insights into how you envision growing through your grief.

Use the space below to write your future self a letter.

_____

_____

_____

_____

_____

_____

_____

_____

_____

_____

_____

_____

You can use conversations with your future self at different points in time to help build a path from your present state to the meaningful future you desire. To help bridge your connection between present and future goals, you can also write letters to your future self and tuck them away until an appropriate time.

Concluding Exercise

As this workbook concludes, it's valuable to reflect on your current traumatic grief symptoms and the key concepts and insights you've now integrated into your personal toolkit. Start by retaking the assessment of your traumatic grief symptoms, which can be found at http://www.newharbinger.com/54926. I also invite you to turn to chapter 1 to reflect on the initial grief goals you wrote when you started the workbook. Reflect on your progress with these grief goals.

Are these goals still relevant in your journey? Yes or no? _____

If yes, what are the skills or tools you learned in this workbook that will help you to continue toward these grief goals?

_____

_____

_____

_____

If no, what are your greatest struggles right now? What are the skills or tools you learned in this workbook that will help you work toward these grief goals?

_____

_____

_____

_____

Reflecting on the various topics you've explored, which tool has proven the most effective for managing intense symptoms of traumatic grief and why?

_____

_____

What are the greatest lessons you've gained from your grief up to this point?

_____

_____

_____

_____

What does your grief need the most right now?

_____

_____

_____

_____

What has been your biggest accomplishment since your loved one died?

_____

_____

_____

_____

While this information is fresh in your mind, identify the workbook chapters or exercises you want to revisit. Why will this information be beneficial for your grief?

_____

_____

_____

_____

_____

_____

_____

_____

_____

_____

Concluding Thoughts

You face a lifelong journey of grief after the sudden or unexpected death of your loved one, but now you have a powerful set of tools and skills to cope, build resilience, and continue growing through your traumatic grief. Although difficult, letting go and grieving the future you could have had with your loved one is part of moving toward healing. This process will create space for new opportunities that can integrate or honor your loved one. It may also create a life that brings about meaning in the activities and relationships you choose to pursue. Take the time to identify new possibilities and connect with future visions while remaining present in the life you are building.

Use the skills and tools you have learned throughout the workbook, including how to cope with acute grief (chapter 2), develop a long-term relationship with your grief (chapter 7), and live with uncertainty (chapter 9), as foundations for your future and guides along the way. While this workbook may be ending, your grief and unwavering love for your loved one is not. Your growth and healing will never stop and will continue to change, evolve, and enhance your life. You have given yourself an immeasurable gift by investing your time and emotional energy into addressing your traumatic grief. As your grief evolves and as you continue to gain additional insights and fine-tune your tools, I encourage you to revisit the chapters and workbook exercises on a regular basis.

Please remember to visit the free tool section of the New Harbinger website (http://www.newharbinger.com/54926). Several of the tools and exercises in this workbook are available online, so you can complete them multiple times to document and continue your healing process.

Most of all, please be patient and compassionate with yourself in your grief. Remember this is a process, and you are not looking for an outcome. Your grief is the ultimate expression of your love. Thank you for working with me in your journey.

Acknowledgements

Thank you to Wendy Millstone and all of the wonderful New Harbinger staff for their support and belief in the importance of this workbook. I am incredibly grateful to Ted Rynearson for his continued mentorship and the opportunity to learn from his expertise. I want to express my utmost gratitude to Daniel Baker, Alex DeSoto, Guity Javid, and Lynn Schilaty for their willingness to provide heartfelt feedback from their personal experiences in service of helping others. I want to thank Leslee Koritzke, Michelle Freridge, Nina Gutin, Patty Phillips, Dawn Sherman, Karen Womick, Cindi Sinnema, and Les McCarthy for their encouragement and support. Finally, nothing I do would be possible without the love, dedication, and hard work from Sandra Herweg.

Additional Resources

This workbook explored a range of topics related to the sudden or unexpected death of your loved one and the impact of traumatic grief. To help you further navigate your loss, this list of resources offers additional guidance and support. Please note this is not a comprehensive list and not all of the resources are specific to traumatic grief.

Books

Auerbach, S. 2017. *I'll Write Your Name on Every Beach*. London, England: Jessica Kingsley Publishers.

Baugher, B., and Jordan, J. 2016. *After Suicide Loss: Coping with Your Grief*. 2nd ed. New Castle, WA: Caring People Press.

Blair, P. 2023. *The Long Grief Journey: How Long-Term Unresolved Grief Can Affect Your Mental Health and What to Do About It*. Naperville, IL: Sourcebooks.

Cacciatore, J. 2017. *Bearing the Unbearable: Love, Loss, and the Heartbreaking Path of Grief*. Somerville, MA: Wisdom Publications.

Cantin, K. 2023. *Where Yellow Flowers Bloom: A True Story of Hope through Unimaginable Loss*. Los Angeles, CA: Precocity Press.

Cruz, D. 2020. *Look Around: A Mother's Journey from Grief and Despair to Healing and Hope*. Independently published.

Didion, J. 2007. *The Year of Magical Thinking*. New York: Vintage Books.

Fine, C. 1999. *No Time to Say Goodbye: Surviving The Suicide Of A Loved One*. New York: Broadway Books.

Janoff-Bulman, R. 2002. *Shattered Assumptions: Toward a New Psychology of Trauma*. New York: Free Press.

Klass, D., and Steffen, E. M. 2017. *Continuing Bonds in Bereavement: New Directions for Research and Practice*. New York: Routledge.

Levine, P. 1997. *Waking the Tiger: Healing Trauma*. Berkeley, CA: North Atlantic Books.

Levine, P. 2005. *Healing Trauma: A Pioneering Program for Restoring the Wisdom of Your Body*. Louisville, CO: Sounds True.

Neff, K., and Germer, C. 2018. *The Mindful Self-Compassion Workbook*. New York: Guilford Press.

Noel, B., and Blair, P. 2008. *I Wasn't Ready to Say Goodbye: Surviving, Coping and Healing After the Sudden Death of a Loved One*. Naperville, IL: Sourcebooks.

O'Connor, M. 2023. *The Grieving Brain: The Surprising Science of How We Learn from Love and Loss*. San Francisco: HarperOne.

Raja, S. 2012. *Overcoming Trauma and PTSD: A Workbook Integrating Skills from ACT, DBT, and CBT*. Oakland, CA: New Harbinger Publications.

Saindon, C. 2014. *Murder Survivor's Handbook: Real-Life Stories, Tips & Resources*. Los Angeles, CA: Wigeon Publishing.

Sausys, A. 2014. *Yoga for Grief Relief: Simple Practices for Transforming Your Grieving Mind and Body*. Oakland, CA: New Harbinger Publications.

Stahl, B., and Goldstein, E. 2019. *A Mindfulness-Based Stress Reduction Workbook*. Oakland, CA: New Harbinger Publications.

Tedeschi, R., and Calhoun, L. 1995. Trauma & Transformation: Growing in the Aftermath of Suffering. Thousand Oaks, CA: SAGE Publications.

Tedeschi, R., and Moore, B. 2016. *The Posttraumatic Growth Workbook: Coming Through Trauma Wiser, Stronger, and More Resilient*. Oakland, CA: New Harbinger Publications.

Van der Kolk, B. 2015. *The Body Keeps the Score: Brain, Mind, and Body in the Healing of Trauma*. New York: Penguin Books.

Podcasts

Grief Out Loud

The Grief Sofa

Grief Unfiltered

How to Deal with Grief and Trauma

The Mindfulness and Grief Podcast

Sudden Bereavement Podcast

Untethered: Healing the Pain from a Sudden Death

What's Your Grief

Organizations

AfterTalk: www.aftertalk.com

Alliance of Hope: www.allianceofhope.org

American Foundation for Suicide Prevention: www.afsp.org

Association for Death Education and Counseling: www.adec.org

The Center for Compassion Focused Therapy: www.mindfulcompassion.com

The Compassionate Friends: www.compassionatefriends.org

Dougy Center: www.dougy.org

Grief Companioning Project: www.griefcompanioning.com

My Grief Connection: www.mygriefconnection.org

Open to Hope: www.opentohope.com

Self-Compassion: www.self-compassion.org

Traumatic Grief Solutions: www.traumaticgriefsolutions.com

What's Your Grief: www.whatsyourgrief.com

References

Bonanno, G. 2004. "Loss, Trauma, and Human Resilience: Have We Underestimated the Human Capacity to Thrive After Extremely Aversive Events?" *American Psychologist* 59(1): 20–28.

Boss, P. 2021. *The Myth of Closure: Ambiguous Loss in a Time of Pandemic and Change.* New York: W.W. Norton & Company.

Braehler, C., and K. Neff. 2020. "Self-Compassion in PTSD." In M. T. Tull & N. A. Kimbrel (Eds.), *Emotion in Posttraumatic Stress Disorder: Etiology, Assessment, Neurobiology, and Treatment* 567–596. Cambridge, MA: Elsevier Academic Press.

Brown, B. 2015. *Rising Strong: How the Ability to Reset Transforms the Way We Live, Love, Parent, and Lead.* New York: Random House.

Burke, B., and E. Rynearson, eds. 2022. *The Restorative Nature of Ongoing Connections with the Deceased: Exploring Presence Within Absence.* New York: Routledge.

Carleton, N., P. Norton, and J. Asmundson. 2007. "Fearing the Unknown: A Short Version of the Intolerance of Uncertainty Scale." *Journal of Anxiety Disorders* 21(1): 105–117.

Clark, D. 2013. "Cognitive Restructuring." In *The Wiley Handbook for Cognitive Behavioral Therapy,* edited by S. Hofmann. Hoboken, NJ: Wiley-Blackwell.

Davis C., D. Lehman, R. Silver, C. Wortman, and J. Ellard. 1996. "Self-Blame Following a Traumatic Event: The Role of Perceived Avoidability." *Personality and Social Psychology Bulletin* 22: 557–567.

Doka, K. J. and A. S. Tucci, eds. 2018. *Transforming Loss: Finding the Potential for Growth.* New York: Routledge.

Field, N. P, and G. Bonanno. 2001. "The Role of Blame in Adaptation in the First Five Years Following the Death of a Spouse." *American Behavioral Scientist* 44: 764–781.

Heintzelman, S. J., and L. A. King. 2019. "Routines and Meaning in Life." *Personality and Social Psychology Bulletin* 45(5): 688–699.

Hershfield, H. 2023. *Your Future Self: How to Make Tomorrow Better Today*. New York: Little, Brown Spark.

Hewson, H., N. Galbraith, C. Jones, and G. Heath. 2023. "The Impact of Continuing Bonds Following Bereavement: A Systematic Review." *Death Studies* 48(10): 1001–1014.

Holland, J., K. Thompson, V. Rozalski, and W. Lichtenthal. 2013. "Bereavement-Related Regret Trajectories Among Widowed Older Adults." *The Journals of Gerontology: Series B* 69B(1): 40–47.

Hutto, D., and S. Gallagher. 2017. "Re-Authoring Narrative Therapy: Improving Our Self-Management Tools." *Philosophy, Psychiatry & Psychology* 24(2), 157–167.

Janoff-Bulman, R. 1992. *Shattered Assumptions: Towards a New Psychology of Trauma*. New York: Free Press.

Kamp, K., E. Steffen, A. Moskowitz, and H. Spindler. 2021. "Prevalence and Phenomenology of Sensory Experiences of a Deceased Spouse: A Survey of Bereaved Older Adults." *OMEGA - Journal of Death and Dying* 87(1), 103–125.

Kauffman, J. 2002. *Loss of the Assumptive World: A Theory of Traumatic Loss*. New York: Brunner-Routledge.

Klass, D., P. Silverman, and S., Nickerson, eds. 1996. *Continuing Bonds: New Understandings of Grief*. New York: Taylor & Francis.

Klass, D., and E. Steffen, eds. 2017. *Continuing Bonds in Bereavement: New Directions for Research and Practice*. New York: Routledge.

Korpela K., U. Kinnunen, S. Geurts, J. de Bloom, and M. Sianoja. 2016. "Recovery During Lunch Breaks: Testing Long-Term Relations with Energy Levels at Work." *Organ Psychology* 1(1): 7.

Kruglanski, A., and D. Webster. 1996. "Motivated Closing of the Mind: 'Seizing' and 'Freezing.'" *Psychological Review* 103(2): 263–283.

Levine, P. 2005. *Healing Trauma: A Pioneering Program for Restoring the Wisdom of Your Body*. Louisville, CO: Sounds True.

Lewinsohn, P., and J. Libet. 1972. "Pleasant Events, Activity Schedules, and Depressions." *Journal of Abnormal Psychology* 79(3): 291–295.

Li, J., M. Stroebe, C. Chan, and A. Chow. 2014. "Guilt in Bereavement: A Review and Conceptual Framework." *Death Studies* 38: 165–171.

Luo, Y., X. Chen, S. Qi, X. You, and X. Huang. 2018. "Well-Being and Anticipation for Future Positive Events: Evidences from an fMRI Study." *Frontiers in Psychology* 8.

Moore, D. 2018. "Expert Companionship: A Framework for Facilitating Posttraumatic Growth." In *Transforming Loss: Finding the Potential for Growth,* edited by K. J. Doka and A. S. Tucci. New York: Routledge.

Neff, K. 2011. *Self-Compassion: The Proven Power of Being Kind to Yourself.* New York: William Morrow.

Noel, B. and P. Blair. 2008. *I Wasn't Ready to Say Goodbye: Surviving, Coping and Healing After the Sudden Death of a Loved One.* Naperville, IL: Sourcebooks.

Rice, A. 2015. "Common Therapeutic Factors in Bereavement Groups." *Death Studies* 39(3): 165–172.

Rynearson, E. 2012. "Invoking an Alliance with the Deceased after Violent Death." In *Techniques of Grief Therapy: Creative Practice for Counseling the Bereaved,* edited by Robert Neimeyer. New York: Taylor & Francis.

Schultz, W. 2016. "Dopamine Reward Prediction Error Coding." *Dialogues in Clinical Neuroscience* 18(1): 23–32.

Siegel, D. 2020. *The Developing Mind: How Relationships and the Brain Interact to Shape Who We Are.* (3rd ed.) New York: Guilford Press.

Smith, K., G. Everly, and G. Haight. 2012. "SAS4: Validation of a Four-Item Measure of Worry and Rumination." *Advances in Accounting Behavioral Research* 15: 101–131.

Stroebe, M., and H. Schut. 1999. "The Dual Process Model of Coping with Bereavement: Rationale and Description." *Death Studies* 23(3): 197–224.

Stroebe, M., W. Stroebe, R. van de Schoot, H. Schut, G. Abakoumkin, and J. Li. 2014. "Guilt in Bereavement: The Role of Self-Blame and Regret in Coping with Loss." *PLoS ONE* 9(5), Article e96606.

Tedeschi, R., and Calhoun, L. 1995. *Trauma and Transformation: Growing in the Aftermath of Suffering.* Thousand Oaks, CA: SAGE Publications.

Tedeschi R., and L. Calhoun. 2004. "Target Article: 'Posttraumatic Growth: Conceptual Foundations and Empirical Evidence.'" *Psychological Inquiry* 15(1): 1–18.

Tonkin, L. 1996. "Growing around Grief—Another Way of Looking at Grief and Recovery." *Bereavement Care* 15(1).

Torges, C., A. Stewart, and S. Nolen-Hoeksema. 2008. "Regret Resolution, Aging, and Adapting to Loss." *Psychology and Aging* 23: 169–180.

Weinberg, N. 1994. "Self-Blame, Other Blame, and Desire for Revenge: Factors in Recovery from Bereavement." *Death Studies* 18(6): 583–593.

Jennifer R. Levin, PhD, LMFT, specializes in traumatic grief, sudden or unexpected death, and trauma. She is a licensed marriage and family therapist, and a recognized fellow in thanatology. Her work includes crisis support after a sudden death for businesses, schools, and communities, and proactive planning for unexpected death to minimize the trauma and grief that occurs when unprepared. Levin is also host of the *Untethered* podcast.

Foreword writer **Edward K. Rynearson, MD**, is a clinical psychiatrist and researcher from Seattle, WA, where he served as clinical professor of psychiatry at the University of Washington. His research focuses on the effects of violent death on family members. He has given national and international trainings on the management of the clinical effects of violent death—establishing an information network for providers, teachers, and researchers of traumatic grief after violent death.

Real change *is* possible

For more than fifty years, New Harbinger has published
proven-effective self-help books and pioneering
workbooks to help readers of all ages and backgrounds
improve mental health and well-being, and achieve lasting
personal growth. In addition, our spirituality books
offer profound guidance for deepening awareness and
cultivating healing, self-discovery, and fulfillment.

Founded by psychologist Matthew McKay and
Patrick Fanning, New Harbinger is proud to be
an independent, employee-owned company.
Our books reflect our core values of integrity, innovation,
commitment, sustainability, compassion, and trust.
Written by leaders in the field and recommended by
therapists worldwide, New Harbinger books are practical,
accessible, and provide real tools for real change.

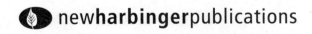 **newharbinger**publications

FROM OUR COFOUNDER—

As cofounder of New Harbinger and a clinical psychologist since 1978, I know that emotional problems are best helped with evidence-based therapies. These are the treatments derived from scientific research (randomized controlled trials) that show what works. Whether these treatments are delivered by trained clinicians or found in a self-help book, they are designed to provide you with proven strategies to overcome your problem.

Therapies that aren't evidence-based—whether offered by clinicians or in books—are much less likely to help. In fact, therapies that aren't guided by science may not help you at all. That's why this New Harbinger book is based on scientific evidence that the treatment can relieve emotional pain.

This is important: if this book isn't enough, and you need the help of a skilled therapist, use the following resources to find a clinician trained in the evidence-based protocols appropriate for your problem. And if you need more support—a community that understands what you're going through and can show you ways to cope—resources for that are provided below, as well.

Real help is available for the problems you have been struggling with. The skills you can learn from evidence-based therapies will change your life.

Matthew McKay, PhD
Cofounder, New Harbinger Publications

**If you need a therapist, the following organization
can help you find a therapist trained in cognitive behavioral therapy (CBT).**

The Association for Behavioral & Cognitive Therapies (ABCT) Find-a-Therapist service offers a list of therapists schooled in CBT techniques. Therapists listed are licensed professionals who have met the membership requirements of ABCT and who have chosen to appear in the directory.
Please visit www.abct.org and click on Find a Therapist.

For additional support:

National Center for PTSD
visit www.ptsd.va.gov

Anxiety and Depression Association of American (ADAA)
Please visit www.adaa.org

The Suicide & Crisis Lifeline
24 hours a day
**If you or someone you love is dealing with a crisis right now, please call
or text 988 or go to 988lifeline.org to reach the Suicide & Crisis Lifeline**

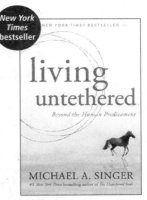

Did you know there are **free tools** you can download for this book?

Free tools are things like **worksheets**, **guided meditation exercises**, and **more** that will help you get the most out of your book.

You can download free tools for this book—whether you bought or borrowed it, in any format, from any source—from the New Harbinger website. All you need is a NewHarbinger.com account. Just use the URL provided in this book to view the free tools that are available for it. Then, click on the "download" button for the free tool you want, and follow the prompts that appear to log in to your NewHarbinger.com account and download the material.

You can also save the free tools for this book to your **Free Tools Library** so you can access them again anytime, just by logging in to your account! Just look for this button on the book's free tools page.

+ Save this to my free tools library

If you need help accessing or downloading free tools, visit **newharbinger.com/faq** or contact us at **customerservice@newharbinger.com**.